Praise for *Reciprocity Rules*

"This truly exciting volume addresses an acute aspect of anthropological field-work: that of reciprocity. As it can be a thorny issue, a systematic inquiry into it has been neglected for far too long. How can, and should, anthropologists give something back to the people who have allowed them into their lives, even into sensitive situations? And for how long should this reciprocity go on? As the editors Michelle C. Johnson and Edmund (Ned) Searles argue, this raises key ethical and methodological issues. Filling an embarrassing gap, *Reciprocity Rules* is bound to become influential."—Helena Wulff, Stockholm University, and author of *Rhythms of Writing: An Anthropology of Irish Literature*

"A very welcome volume about that fundamental question within anthropological fieldwork: how do we compensate our hosts? Based on the extensive long-term fieldwork experiences of the authors and richly illustrated with telling ethnographic details, the chapters convincingly and insightfully demonstrate the importance of a nuanced understanding of reciprocal fieldwork obligations. Topics such as the importance of studying local gifting practices, the pros and cons of different kinds of gifts and support, the importance of nonmaterial forms of compensation, the obligations—and joys—of fictive kinship relationships, reciprocal writing strategies, the context of decolonization, and many more each exemplify the essential ethical and moral fieldwork lessons that can be learned from this original volume. Highly recommended for classes in ethnographic research methods."—Geert Mommersteeg, University of Utrecht, and author of *In the City of the Marabouts: Islamic Culture in West Africa*

"*Reciprocity Rules* is a great contribution to our understanding of fieldwork. Applying 'the Gift' and 'reciprocity' in concrete and reflexive ways, this collection portrays the inside story of how relations between ethnographers and those they are working with actually develop over time. Like all close relationships, those in the field engage challenges and misunderstandings as well as treasures of deep connection. Based on diverse fieldwork across three continents, the book's authors average twenty-four years of connection with their field communities. For those interested in the ethics, methods, and experience of fieldwork, including junior scholars, this work is a gold mine of concrete and practical insights that reach far beyond the standard generalities of research design and methods."—Bruce Knauft, Samuel C. Dobbs Professor of Anthropology, Emory University, and author of *The Gebusi: Lives Transformed in a Rainforest World*

"The problematics of reciprocity unify this stimulating collection. Its contributors illustrate, as chapter 1 succinctly puts it, how fieldwork is 'a fundamentally relational endeavor' and—crucially—how anthropologists 'owe our expertise to the bundles of relations that make, and have made, our knowledge possible.' Recognizing the depth of those debts and the colonial histories that enabled them, the chapters converge around an understanding of anthropological knowledge as emergent from asymmetrical social exchanges among persons. The expertise anthropologists claim has never been simply our own. Our knowledge practices and products are therefore only as ethically sustainable and epistemologically valuable as our capacity to honor and renew the agreements on which they rest."—Rena S. Lederman, Princeton University

"A brilliant and moving intervention into the fraught but fecund terrain of encounter between anthropologist and interlocutor, researcher and host community, and a profound set of meditations on the ethics of such engagement. Trail-blazing in its treatment of the unstated in anthropological fieldwork, this book should be required reading for fieldworkers, not only in anthropology but in all the qualitative research disciplines."—Charles D. Piot, Duke University, and author of *The Fixer: Visa Lottery Chronicles*

"These vivid and frank stories take us to the heart of ethical challenges in long-term fieldwork and show us how we must learn—and relearn—ways to reciprocate in ongoing, caring relationships."—Kirin Narayan, Australian National University, and author of *Everyday Creativity: Singing Goddesses in the Himalayan Foothills*

Reciprocity Rules

Reciprocity Rules

Friendship and Compensation in Fieldwork Encounters

Edited by
Michelle C. Johnson
Edmund (Ned) Searles

LEXINGTON BOOKS
Lanham • Boulder • New York • London

Published by Lexington Books
An imprint of The Rowman & Littlefield Publishing Group, Inc.
4501 Forbes Boulevard, Suite 200, Lanham, Maryland 20706
www.rowman.com

6 Tinworth Street, London SE11 5AL, United Kingdom

British Library Cataloguing in Publication Information Available

Library of Congress Cataloging-in-Publication Data

Names: Johnson, Michelle C., 1970– editor. | Searles, Edmund (Ned), 1967– editor.
Title: Reciprocity rules : friendship and compensation in fieldwork encounters / edited by Michelle C. Johnson, Edmund (Ned) Searles.
Description: Lanham, Maryland : Lexington Books, 2021. | Includes bibliographical references and index. | Summary: "Focusing on compensation, friendship, and collaboration, this book explores what anthropologists and research participants give to each other in and beyond fieldwork. Contributors argue that while learning and following the local rules of reciprocity are challenging, they are essential to responsible research and efforts to decolonize anthropology."—Provided by publisher.
Identifiers: LCCN 2020039350 (print) | LCCN 2020039351 (ebook) | ISBN 9781498592949 (cloth) | ISBN 9781498592956 (epub)
ISBN 9781498592963 (pbk)
Subjects: LCSH: Anthropology—Fieldwork | Interpersonal relations.
Classification: LCC GN34.3.F53 R43 2021 (print) | LCC GN34.3.F53 (ebook) | DDC 301.072/3—dc23
LC record available at https://lccn.loc.gov/2020039350
LC ebook record available at https://lccn.loc.gov/2020039351

To all of those who taught us—with kindness, patience, and humor—the rules of reciprocity

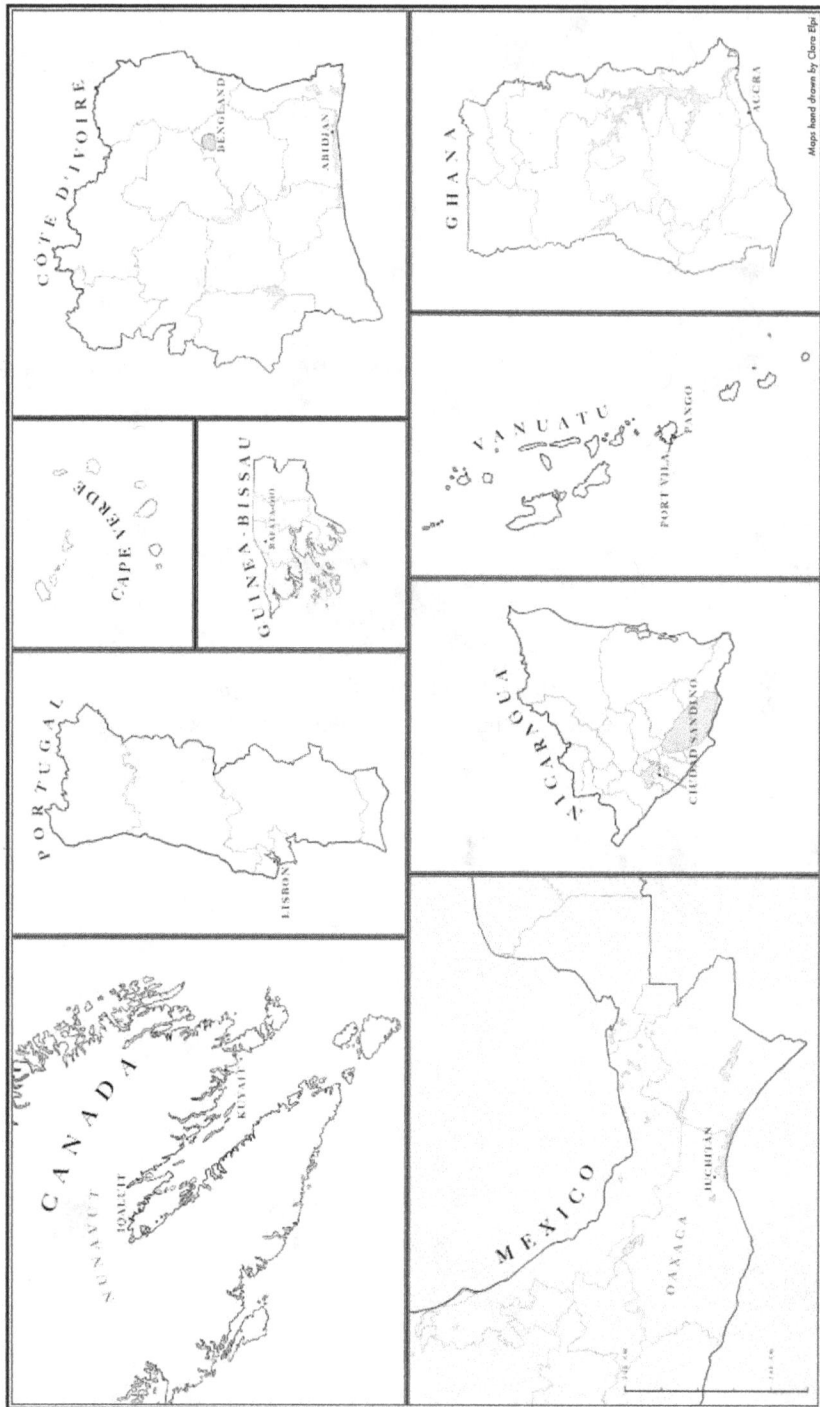

Maps Indicating Fieldsites Highlighted in the Chapters. *Source:* Maps hand drawn by Clara Elpi.

Contents

List of Figures

Introduction

Michelle C. Johnson and Edmund (Ned) Searles

ETHICS AND COMPENSATION BEYOND THE IRB

This volume was inspired by two distinct sources at the intersection of teaching and research. First, the coeditors regularly teach the qualitative methodology course, "Field Research in Local Communities," required for anthropology majors at their home institution, Bucknell University. In addition to learning about and practicing the various methods that anthropologists employ in their research, students devise and conduct their own semester-long ethnographic research project in the local community. In preparation for this challenging undertaking, students learn about all aspects of the research process, including ethics and how to navigate Bucknell's Institutional Review Board (IRB). As one of the course requirements, students take the online research ethics certification course (Collaborative Institutional Training Initiative, or CITI) that faculty and students working with human subjects must complete before conducting research that will involve the dissemination of generalizable results. The online course traces the origins and development of research ethics in the United States by examining a series of infamous case studies, such as the Stanford Prison Experiment and the Tearoom Trade study.[1]

Although the CITI course covers many crucial issues and raises some important questions pertaining to research, it possesses, as Rena Lederman (2016:46) puts it, a profound "tone-deafness concerning disciplinary differences." She (2016:43) explains:

> As a research method employed in different ways in sociocultural anthropology and other fields, ethnographic fieldwork (participant observation particularly) is a poor fit with the biomedically rooted assumptions about methodologically competent, ethically responsible research that inform human-subjects research

regulations . . . fieldwork's epistemological value depends on the cultivation of multidimensional relationships between investigators and their interlocutors, and on the quality of investigator openness to socially situated contingencies.

As one example of this "poor fit," the CITI course draws a particular model of ethics—one that maximizes the benefits of the research while minimizing harm to research participants—that rarely, if ever, aligns with the complicated and often confusing rules of reciprocity that anthropologists encounter in the course of long-term fieldwork, especially in settings other than the United States.

Adding to its limited usefulness for ethnographic research, the CITI course questions but ultimately endorses a model in which "research subjects" are treated as means to an end (i.e., a source of data for scholarly "products," such as books and articles) rather than ends themselves (i.e., individuals with their own values, priorities, and goals), a distinction many anthropologists find problematic. As Joan Cassell (1980:32) states:

> A more appropriate ethical framework for judging fieldwork might be constructed upon respect for individual autonomy based on the fundamental principle that persons always be treated as ends in themselves, never merely as means—the Kantian categorical imperative.

Indeed, as Lederman (2016:53–4) explains, anthropologists become entangled with those they strive to understand through their research, and in the process, "subjects" become more like teachers, consultants, collaborators, and hosts and, as the contributors of this volume contend, sometimes even co-authors, friends, and "family."

At Bucknell University, IRB discussions regarding human subjects focus almost exclusively on compensation as how much money researchers can pay their "subjects," whether that payment is taxable, and how to report payments to the IRS. Absent from these discussions are broader concerns about ethical forms of "payment" in diverse cultural settings, the appropriateness of alternative, non-monetary forms of compensation, such as gifts in kind, and the possibility of doing "some good" in the community where one conducts research, a point that Fluehr-Lobban (2003a:226) emphasizes: " [I]instead of conceiving the ethical treatment of humans in research as doing no harm, the complementary invocation to do some good represents a conscious step toward an ethically conscious, proactive shift in research methods."

Anthropologists are increasingly engaging in critical discussions about the IRB's shortcomings in addressing the uniqueness of ethnographic research. For example, Diane Duclos (2019) argues that guidelines for ethical research set by the IRB do not account for those situations in which anthropologists need to identify research participants by name. In writing this volume, we join Duclos and others in critically assessing the shortcomings of IRB guidelines for ethnographic research, especially when thinking about how to best compensate research subjects in long-term fieldwork.

The second source of inspiration for this volume was a panel at the Society for Applied Anthropology meetings in Santa Fe, New Mexico in 2017. Driving the panel was a realization regarding how anthropologists generally talk and write about compensation, friendship, and reciprocity in long-term ethnographic fieldwork. For example, they often engage in casual conversations about these topics with colleagues over dinner or in the informal meeting spaces of universities and academic conferences. They mention these issues sporadically in short sections of books, articles, newsletters, or fieldwork memoirs. Consider the following example from a newsletter article by Andrew Strathern, (1983:6) "Research in Papua New Guinea, Cross-currents of Conflict":

> The problem of reciprocity . . . resolves itself into two points: one, reciprocity must be *long-term*, and two, reciprocity must operate at many *different levels* over time. That we do not, or cannot, or will not, attain these ideals is not just regrettable: it poses a considerable danger to the future accessibility of areas for fieldwork to be practiced in at all. It should therefore be of concern to the institutions as well as to individuals. (original italics)

Consider also this example from Geert Mommersteeg's (2012:16) book, *In the City of the Marabouts*:

> The success or failure of anthropological fieldwork depends on the kind of relationship fieldworkers manage to establish with the people in whose city, village, or group they temporarily reside. The important thing is the interaction, the rapport between researchers and their hosts. The recognition of the fundamentally human character of the undertaking is indispensable to its success.

While insights such as these are both inspirational and informative, rarely, if ever, do they constitute the central theme of anthropologists' scholarly works. Determined to shift discussions about compensation, friendship, and reciprocity in anthropological fieldwork from hallways and restaurants to more formal scholarly spaces, Michelle Johnson organized the panel, "Trails of Reciprocity: Compensation, Friendship, and Helping in Fieldwork Encounters," which highlighted the centrality of these themes to anthropologists' fieldwork, scholarly works, and personal lives. The current volume emerged from the enlightening scholarly exchange that ensued. When the opportunity to publish the conference panel as an edited volume arose unexpectedly, four of the session's presenters agreed to expand their papers into full-length chapters. Michelle recruited two additional scholars who were not part of the original session but were delighted to contribute chapters to the volume. Finally, our discussant on the panel, Alma Gottlieb, enthusiastically agreed to write the afterword.

Rather than treating ethics exclusively, or even primarily, as an IRB-mandated set of research dos and don'ts, and compensation as monetary payments that may (or may not) be taxable, contributors of this volume consider these topics as complex and dynamic processes—the rules of reciprocity—that anthropologists must learn within the specific moral environments in which they work. In long-term anthropological fieldwork, ethics involves cultivating intense and long-lasting personal relationships, sometimes, friendships, and even "family" relations, with many different kinds of individuals and negotiating these relationships over time. Complicating matters further, local community members may even deem the behavior of some of these individuals as unethical, as several of this volume's chapters reveal. Following Luke Lassiter's lead, our contributors highlight that long-term fieldwork involves a specific form of collaboration between researchers and research participants, and it requires negotiating an ongoing series of moral co-commitments, "consensual agreements . . . that provide the base for the project's particular evolution as a cooperative undertaking." (Lassiter 2005a:97) We believe that in the course of their research, anthropologists accumulate a debt to their research participants. What this debt looks like specifically or how it should be repaid, however, is complex and not always clear in the beginning. It also might change considerably over time as anthropologists and their hosts move through the life course and encounter opportunities or obstacles. We argue here that anthropologists must acknowledge this debt: they must talk about it openly with research participants, host communities, and other scholars. Furthermore, like the contributors of this volume, they should write about it, in all of its complexity.

LEARNING THE RULES OF RECIPROCITY

Reciprocity is a dominant theme in the history of anthropological theory and remains a key research topic of economic anthropology. Mauss's classic study of the social and cultural dimensions of exchange in non-Western settings, *The Gift*, aimed to understand the myriad meanings and functions attached to the reciprocal exchange of goods, including gifts that are "obligatorily given and received." (Mauss 2015:57) According to Mauss, "gifts" are "total social phenomena" that "[express] all at once and at a stroke all sorts of institutions: religious, judicial, and ethical (morale)—these being political and familial at the same time; economic . . . aesthetic." (2015:58) Indeed, a central question driving Mauss's analysis was, "What force is there in the thing one gives that compels the recipient to return it?" (Mauss 2105:58) Bronislaw Malinowski, another of anthropology's key historic figures, wrote: "Giving for the sake of giving is one of the most important features of Trobriand sociology, and, from its very general and fundamental nature . . . a universal feature of all primitive societies" (cited in Gudeman 2001:84). A more contemporary theorist, Marshall Sahlins, argues that reciprocity is the "building block of exchange, economy, and society" (cited in Gudeman 2001:86).

Despite anthropologists' recognition of the crucial role of reciprocity in building not only social relationships, even entire societies, they have been slow to consider their own participation in the total social phenomenon of gift-giving and other forms of reciprocity as they play out in the fieldwork process. This is curious, especially given discussions about the power of reciprocity to extend beyond individual communities, incorporating "others" across time and space. As Gudeman (2001:86) astutely observes:

> Reciprocity is never contained within a community. The gift and reciprocity are used to probe across its borders, for a variety of motives, such as establishing mutuality and peace, expressing dominance, manipulating to advantage, displaying power and wealth, and bringing new members. The gift is an experiment in making community.

This collection of chapters aims to address this shortcoming. Specifically, contributors explore the role of reciprocity in creating community between anthropologists and their research participants over time. In so doing, they seek to better understand how anthropologists become interwoven into complex webs of reciprocity that organize and inform the ways in which local people relate to one other, as well as to the wider world.

Building on Lassiter's (2005a:97) concept of ethnography as an ongoing and negotiated process of moral co-commitments, this volume focuses on the co-commitments that are expressed through friendship and compensation in and beyond fieldwork. Friendship and compensation, we argue, both inform and are informed by local rules of reciprocity. As an important dimension of ethics in research, reciprocity is one of the ethical principles listed in the code of ethics of the American Anthropological Association. The 2009 version of the code (Section III.A.6) highlights anthropologists' debt to the members of the communities in which they work, as well as their obligation to compensate them in appropriate ways:

> While anthropologists may gain personally from their work, they must not exploit individuals, groups, animals, or cultural or biological materials. They

should recognize their debt to societies in which they work and their obligation
to reciprocate with people studied in appropriate ways

While the word "reciprocity" appeared in the 2009 version of the code,
it was, interestingly, removed from the 2012 revised version. This decision
might reflect the sentiment among some scholars (e.g., Pink, 1998) that the
rules of reciprocity in anthropological research are so dynamic and complex
that they are difficult, if not impossible, to codify. Furthermore, it speaks to
the challenge that anthropologists must continually revisit and even revise the
rules of reciprocity at various times throughout the research process. As the
revised code states: "Determinations regarding what is in the best interests
of others or what kinds of efforts are appropriate to increase well-being are
value-laden and should reflect sustained discussion with others concerned."
As anthropologists who conduct long-term fieldwork learn through a range
of different encounters and experiences, the rules of reciprocity involve much
more than simply deciding how much to pay subjects for their time and
knowledge, especially in contexts in which, as Gail Wagoner (n.d.) writes,
"knowledge or ownership is communal, widespread, or not a commodity."
Wagoner (n.d.) continues that in such contexts "anthropologists must seek
individual solutions."

In sharing what sociologist John Van Maanen (2011) refers to as "tales
from the field," contributors to this volume reflect on their own experiences
with friendship, reciprocity, and compensation in long-term ethnographic
fieldwork. These include assessing both successes and failures in forging
meaningful and enduring ties to the communities in which they work, and
cultivating friendships or "family" ties that persist long after the researcher
returns home and that are often transformative for both parties. As Piers
Vitebsky writes:

> One of the main effects of long-term fieldwork is the deepening of friend-
> ships. . . as the anthropologist is normalized from freak visitor to a recurrent
> presence. For a few local people who become our special friends, their closeness
> may profoundly change their lives as well as our own. (2012:184)

Contributors to this volume narrate their attempts at not only learning the
local rules of reciprocity, but the challenges of attempting to adhere to them
over time. Some report that they eventually discovered, for example, that their
efforts at making friends and behaving ethically were not interpreted as such
by members of their host communities. Others recount how the local rules of
reciprocity, which they thought they had mastered during earlier periods of
fieldwork, had changed after many decades, revealing new and unexpected

opportunities for collaboration and other forms of moral co-commitments. Still others confess that their idealized notions of reciprocity, friendship, and compensation became difficult, even impossible, to sustain over time given changing political conditions, economic or personal constraints, and professional conventions, such as academic publishing. Many of the authors report that their efforts at friendship or reciprocity have never felt—and perhaps never will feel—adequate. In recounting their varied experiences, contributors expose the highly contextualized and nuanced nature of friendship, compensation, and reciprocity in long-term ethnographic fieldwork.

Building on scholarly works addressing the intense and often ambivalent emotions that accompany anthropology's hallmark method of participant observation (e.g., Hume and Mulcock, 2004; Goulet and Miller, 2007; Howell and Talle, 2012b; Kan, 2001; McLean and Leibing, 2007; Davies and Spencer, 2010), contributors to this volume also address how the challenges of learning and following the rules of reciprocity in local contexts sometimes converge and at other times conflict with culturally specific notions of friendship and family. James Carrier (1999:21) defines *friendship* as "a kind of relationship, one based on spontaneous and unconstrained sentiment or affection." This relationship is, furthermore, mediated by various structural factors, such as race, ethnicity, gender, and class, as well as by personal factors, such as personality. In the context of fieldwork, treating knowledge as a commodity can potentially enhance or undermine friendships, depending on the context. For example, when Ned Searles asked if he could pay his host family for the food that he was told to take freely from the refrigerator whenever he wanted, his host "father" responded in a frustrated tone, "I thought we were friends." What Ned intended as a gesture of friendship and reciprocity, his host father interpreted as an affront to one of the most central notions of Inuit culture: one's possessions must be shared freely with others. For Michelle, returning to the field itself is an important form of non-monetary reciprocity. The idea of how returns to one's fieldsite shapes the anthropologist's relationship to members of the communities in which they work is an overarching theme of Signe Howell and Aud Talle's (2012) volume, *Returns to the Field*. As Bruce Knauft (2012:258) writes in the volume's afterword:

> The long-term ethnographer often accumulates not just increasing status as an aficionado or historian of the people she or he studies among, but increasing potentials for friendship and supporting local communities. At turns loving, moral, humanitarian, stressful, demanding, these ties are often both very rich and refractory to comparative assessment. They go beyond professional connections, within-culture friendships, humanitarian interventions, or even familial, much less contractual, obligations.

In shaping the relationships that anthropologists cultivate and manage in long-term fieldwork and throughout their professional careers, the rules of reciprocity regarding friendship and compensation are difficult to isolate, since they are often bound up with other analytical categories. Breaking the rules can also have varied consequences, depending on the context at hand. Compensating a research participant for collaboration on a project may solidify a friendship or it might threaten the precarious boundary between a friendship and a professional, working relationship. Friendship and compensation may also find more appropriate expression, as some of our contributors demonstrate, through non-material forms, such as the gift of a name bestowed on a researcher. A gifted name can serve as a point of entry into larger kinship networks whose members provide support to the researcher but from whom the researcher can also learn about the rules of reciprocity that bind together community members as a whole (see Counts and Counts, 1998).

Another of the volume's contributors, Carolyn Rouse, discusses how she decided to reciprocate the hospitality that her research participants extended to her by building a public high school. She later learned, however, that community members did not consider this as a gift or an expression of reciprocity, but rather as a fulfillment of the obligation to give to them what they believe everyone should have, but which they lacked: the fundamental human right to a free and equal education. Other contributors, such as Chelsea Wentworth and her host "sister," Julie Kalsrap, take up the theme of equality more explicitly, exploring the ways in which the culture of academia—including academic publishing conventions—limit anthropologists' ability to compensate research participants in ways that allow them to achieve the same status and opportunities as those enjoyed by anthropologists themselves.

Learning and following the rules of reciprocity in any society are complicated by the fact that members of local communities are increasingly hiring anthropologists to assist them in finding solutions for locally identified problems, and even to advocate on their behalf. While some anthropologists purposefully enter into an advocacy relationship with their host communities—for example, by providing expert testimony in court proceedings—others find themselves in this role by accident or circumstance (e.g., Kirsch, 2018). And yet, beyond the formal requirements and expectations of university IRBs, friendship, compensation, and reciprocity remain relatively under-theorized and under-analyzed dimensions of anthropological inquiry. As Gary Robinson (2004:154) states:

> The formation of ties of dependence and reciprocity between researcher and subjects, the researcher's incorporation into social groups, and the sometimes gut-wrenching sundering of ties as he or she disengages from research subjects constitutes largely unexplored terrain in analyses of ethnographic fieldwork.

This remains as true today as it was in 2004, as only a small number of anthropologists have addressed these themes explicitly (e.g., Fluehr-Lobban, 2003b; Bell and Coleman, 1999; Gottlieb and Graham, 1994; Gottlieb and Graham, 2012; Powdermaker, 1966). Even in works that address reciprocity explicitly, it is rarely the main focus of analysis. In *Returns to the Field* (Howell and Talle, 2012b), for example, the term "reciprocity" appears in just two of the volume's nine chapters in addition to the afterword. *Reciprocity Rules* extends these important and illuminating studies of long-term fieldwork by concentrating on the rules of reciprocity, compensation, and friendship so as to encourage the next generation of fieldworkers to engage more critically with these issues before, during, and after they complete their fieldwork.

OUTLINE OF THE CHAPTERS

In the chapters that follow, contributors to this volume share stories from their fieldwork, which, in some cases, spans several decades. Their stories provide important insights into the cultural specificity and dynamic nature of the rules of reciprocity that are often not experienced or simply overlooked in shorter fieldwork periods. All of the volume's seven contributors are cultural anthropologists at various stages of their careers. Each has conducted fieldwork in a single site or in multiple, connected sites over an extended period of time. They reflect on the issues of friendship, compensation, and "helping," and how these played out in particular episodes in and beyond their fieldwork. They also discuss how these issues developed and changed over time. Taken as a whole, the research settings span three continents (Africa, North America, and Oceania) and eight countries (Canada, Côte d'Ivoire, Guinea-Bissau, Ghana, Mexico, Nicaragua, Portugal, and Vanuatu).

Chapter 1 sheds light on the unpredictability of relationships cultivated through long-term fieldwork. Josh Fisher describes how he used his friendly connections with the leadership of a U.S.-based NGO to support a local initiative to start a textile manufacturing and export business in Nicaragua. When the NGO's director suddenly broke his commitment to support the fledgling business, loading even more debt and disappointment onto a community already in desperate need of jobs and money, he became known locally as a "scorpion." Fisher tells a story in which there are no simple heroes or villains: it is too easy, he argues, to assign blame to individuals when larger, global forces undermine both anthropologists' and research participants' efforts to overcome the devastating effects of poverty.

In chapter 2, Michelle Johnson recounts how she learned midway through her early fieldwork in rural Guinea-Bissau, West Africa, that a holy man had allegedly anticipated her and her husband's arrival in a prophetic dream. As a result of this dream, the villagers felt obligated to host the foreign couple and treat them because it was the couple's destiny to do "great things" for the village. Johnson reflects on the anthropologist's predestined responsibility to "help," how this expectation unfolded over time, and how her efforts to reciprocate her research participants' help and hospitality were later constrained by political and economic realities as Guinea-Bissau struggled through a civil war, thereby forcing her to begin a new project with Guinean immigrants in Lisbon, Portugal. She argues that although non-material forms of reciprocity should not replace material forms, anthropologists should treat them as equally important forms of compensation.

In chapter 3, Carolyn Rouse explores how race and history may complicate the meaning of an anthropologist's "gift"—in her case, the construction of a high school for the inhabitants of a village near Ghana's capital city, Accra. Considering the value that Ghanaians place on education, and the numerous stories that Rouse heard from her research participants concerning their struggles to pay for their children's transportation and school fees, she could not have imagined a more culturally appropriate gift. She soon learned, however, that her research participants did not consider the school a "gift" but, rather, an attempt to address the inequalities that exist between the Global North and the Global South. Back in the United States, Rouse's academic peers interpreted the gift of a school as an example of neocolonialism. In telling her story, Rouse challenges scholars who assume that development efforts are viewed as gifts by those on the receiving end. She considers what happens when local people are unable to reciprocate and argues that this conundrum exacerbates and solidifies power inequalities around the world.

In chapter 4, Anya Peterson Royce describes how receiving the Medalla Binniza in recognition of her scholarly work on the history, culture, and language of the Isthmus Zapotec helped her understand more clearly the relationship that develops between anthropologists and the people who welcome them into their lives. Royce contends that long-term fieldwork spanning decades brings challenges, status changes, the ability to find new patterns and ask new questions, the opportunity to experience real-time change and a more activist role, and the courage to find one's own voice. She tells the story of how she and her research participants have grown in their understanding of one another, specifically, and in the human condition, more generally.

In chapter 5, Edmund (Ned) Searles shares the valuable insights he learned when deciding how best to compensate his Inuit host family during his fieldwork in the Canadian Arctic. Although his research fellowship was supposed to cover his research and living expenses for nine months of fieldwork, he soon learned that it was not enough to pay for rent much less the wages of research assistants and interviewees. Instead, Searles provided his host family with compensation in kind, including a snowmobile and hunting equipment that the family used to travel to and from their outpost camp located a half a day's journey from the town of Iqaluit. These non-monetary forms of compensation thrust Searles into an extensive network of "family" relationships in which he learned to live according to Inuit rules of reciprocity, experiences that proved crucial to his understanding of the cultural and economic challenges facing contemporary Inuit.

In chapter 6, Chelsea Wentworth and Julie Kalsrap turn a critical and reflective gaze toward the anthropological trope of adoption into a host family. Responding to the challenge of feminist anthropologists and indigenous scholars to recognize and mitigate the power inequalities that fictive kinship relationships in the field can reproduce, Wentworth describes her relationship with her host "sister," Julie Kalsrap—the chapter's coauthor—in the village in which she worked in Vanuatu. Kalsrap then describes this relationship from her own perspective and in her native language, Bislama, highlighting the meaning of "family" and the culturally specific dimensions of kinship relationships and expectations. Together, Wentworth and Kalsrap argue that creating a culture of research and publication that empowers all participants equally is crucial to the decolonization of research practices and to the discipline of anthropology as a whole.

Collectively, the voices and perspectives of these diverse authors reflecting on long-term fieldwork highlight the cultural dimensions and varied meanings of the intersecting and overlapping themes of friendship and compensation, and the rules of reciprocity that shape and are shaped by them. They also highlight new challenges to these rules, intensified by the ever-expanding challenges posed by an ever-increasing gap between the rich and the poor at home and abroad. These challenges only highlight, we contend, the important need, even responsibility, of anthropologists to bring discussions about reciprocity to the forefront of our research, personal lives, and published works.

NOTE

1. We would like to thank Kasey Beduhn at Lexington, who took an interest in this project from the very beginning (when it was a panel at the Society for Applied Anthropology meetings), envisioning it as a book before we did. We are grateful for her vision, as well as her confidence, encouragement, and patience as we accepted her challenge. We are also indebted to Alma Gottlieb, our discussant on the original panel, who not only graciously agreed to write the volume's afterword, but also generously read and commented on every single chapter. The book is better as a result of her efforts. Finally, we would like to thank the anonymous reviewer for pushing us to sharpen the focus and argument; Martin White, for expertly compiling the index; and Clara Elpi, for her creativity and vision in hand-drawing the maps.

Chapter 1

Brother to a Scorpion

Making Anthropological Obligations Visible in Urban Nicaragua

Josh Fisher

MARTA'S WARNING

I didn't know that Roger was a scorpion.[1]

In the 1970s, he was a seminary student, contemplating becoming a minister in the Presbyterian Church. In the 1980s, he was a community organizer, running a soup kitchen and homeless shelter in Statesville, North Carolina. Later, he was a U.S. election observer bearing witness to clandestine U.S. interference in Nicaragua. In the 1990s, during the Gulf War in Iraq, he was a "human shield," a position that required certain skills he learned during the Nicaraguan Contra War. In the summer of 2017, at the age of sixty-seven—about the age of my parents—retirement was not an option. He planned to "die with his boots on" in his role as the director of the Center for Sustainable Development (CSD), a small international aid organization that came into being when in 1994 he and the cofounders of the Statesville project decided to shift their focus to Central America.

Apparently, this is when he started to turn into a scorpion, as my friend Marta tells it. She broke the news to me one day when we were waiting at a bus stop in Ciudad Sandino, a densely populated urban encampment located just west of Nicaragua's capital city of Managua, where Marta, Roger, and I were each living. She knew that Roger and I were friends, and so she tried to broach the topic delicately: "Look at what he does, not what he says. He says he wants to help, but when you turn away, that's when he stings you."

I didn't believe Marta at first, and I'm still not sure I do. But I have learned to appreciate why she would make such a claim, for she had no reason to believe otherwise. "You don't start a non-profit unless you're expecting to make money," she said. Marta held a common suspicion of international NGOs in Nicaragua. They claim goodwill, but they are also unelected representatives of communities that deal in relatively large sums of money, thus giving cause for skepticism. By calling Roger out, Marta believed she could alert others to the potential dangers he presented. By gauging how I reacted, moreover, she could make sure that I wasn't a scorpion, too.

In Nicaragua, scorpions are capitalists: antisocial, antagonistic, incapable of friendship, and uncaring for that which gives them life. They are paradigmatically *salvaje* (savage) creatures, models of antihuman beings that hold a mirror to our social nature (Nading and Fisher, 2018). Like other metaphorical comparisons between human beings and nonhuman others, *scorpionism* is the expression of a critical challenge, a vernacular that identifies those behaviors that violate the social and moral norms of a community.

NGO staffers often invite the criticism when they insist on professional distance, or when they treat living relationships as instruments for advancing their own personal or professional objectives. International organizations like the CSD are particularly susceptible to the critique because their actions are refracted across multiple degrees of social distance. Even an innocent gesture like snapping a photo for the next newsletter may become a lightning rod for such accusations. For the NGO, it may be a necessary part of the work, because donors respond to photographic evidence of injustice. For the person on the other side of the lens, however, it often appears as though NGOs traffic in other people's stories in order to enrich themselves.

Anthropologists may also act like scorpions, I think, when they approach ethnography as a form of "data collection" rather than meaningful and meaning-generating social engagement. Many anthropologists begin their transformation into scorpions when they professionalize. From conducting research and publishing to earning a degree, getting a job, and seeking tenure and promotion, we celebrate steps along the way as personal achievements. But when framed as individuated phenomena, they are illusory. They are professional fetishisms in the sense that the relationships that constitute them—all the debts, influences, and fleeting connections that provide insights, give inspiration, shape research trajectories, and define careers—are recessed from view so that the author may remain intact.

Scorpions, as my Nicaraguan interlocutors advise, fail to recognize these relationships, refuse to repay their social debts, and sometimes leverage their status and position to compel things from others. Above all, they treat relationships as a resource for information, rather than a point of connection. In urban contexts like Ciudad Sandino, Nicaraguans know that people may even become famous, successful, and (relatively) wealthy by publishing books based on other people's knowledge, and yet anthropologists do not share those resources or even acknowledge that others make their careers possible.[2]

By contrast, good anthropologists—and good people—understand that living relationships make knowledge, people, and careers. While some anthropologists professionalize *well* precisely because they feel immune to such debts, being a good anthropologist requires, first and foremost, a willingness to be in another's debt, to feel the force of that debt as it compels its own recognition and reciprocation. This "response-ability" is a necessary precondition of any kind of engagement with the world (Haraway 2008:71).

In this chapter, I explore "giving back" as an integral part of the ethnographic method, and I take as my starting point Marta's warning that everyone contains within them the potential to become a scorpion. On the surface, the warning mirrors ethnographic accounts of antisocial behavior in a cross-cultural perspective. Witchcraft, for instance, has long been interpreted as a commentary on the social ills of unchecked self-interest (Englund, 1996; Evans-Pritchard, 1937; Federici, 2004; Taussig, 1980). But Marta's statement also serves as an invitation to rethink fieldwork in a relational perspective. In social, political, and even evolutionary theory, the figure of the social atom, or the ontological priority imputed to the individual as the basic unit in modern thought, has been subject to extensive critique (Dumont, 1986; Levins and Lewontin, 1985; Maturana and Varela, 1987; Young, 1990). In response, scholars have renewed their commitment to explore practices of commoning and "being-in-common" (Bollier and Helfrich, 2015; Gibson-Graham, 2006; Roelvink et al., 2015; see also Nancy, 1991), to understand people, things, and events such as lines, trajectories, or "bundles of relations" rather than individuated entities (Barad, 2007; Bell, 2017; Ingold 2011:131; Kockelman, 2013; Strathern, 1999), and to advance a relational ontology based on the principle that "nothing preexists the relations that constitute it." (Escobar 2018:101) Early on, feminist thinkers argued that ethnographic research should be conceptualized as something that happens "with" or "alongside" our participants rather than "on" them (e.g., Abu-Lughod, 1990; Behar, 1993). But we have not yet arrived, as a discipline, at a point in which fieldwork itself is understood and described as a fundamentally relational endeavor. The fact remains that fieldwork is an interrelation and interdependence through and through, always and from the beginning. In all cases, ethnography requires that we make visible those relations that make it possible.

A relational perspective also serves to push the discussion about ethnographic methods beyond matters of technique to consider important political and ethical questions: To whom are we obligated? What do we owe? Just how do we "give back"? And how should we negotiate ties that bind us, not merely to our research participants as a homogeneous whole, but, increasingly, to different groups whose members sometimes have divergent or incompatible interests? Going to or returning from "the field," in this perspective, is never as straightforward as it seems, in part because it is no

longer a place on a map. It is an indeterminate space of complex and contradictory connections, commitments, obligations, and other engagements, often
spanning great social, political, economic, or geographic distances, in which
ethnographic fieldworkers willingly and self-consciously enmesh themselves.
This act of "self-entanglement" (*enredarse*, in Spanish, see Alvarez, 2009;
Ribeiro and Escobar, 2015) is generative of knowledge not despite these
tensions, these uncertainties, but in no small part because of them—because
this plural "field of relations" continually makes and remakes our attitudes,
practices, understandings, worldviews, and selves.

The term *relation* is, of course, an overly encompassing yet usefully particular term, containing within it the capacity to signal all manner of social,
emotional, intellectual, or material connection. In this chapter, I follow in
the footsteps of Marilyn Strathern (1988, 1999) and foreground the constitu-
tive force of *exchange* in both making (academic) persons and conducting
ethnographic fieldwork. Some have framed "giving back" as a strategy for
building rapport and thus gaining knowledge (Bernard 2011:277; Schensul
et al., 1999:175), but this instrumental understanding of the deeply social
dimensions of field research is both cynical and exploitable.[3] As we make
connections in the field, and as we accrue debts with many different kinds of
people, we place ourselves in the midst of a complex set of social exchanges.
"Giving back" is the logical consequence of those exchanges, and hence a
necessary component of the ethnographic method.

To be sure, those debts can push and pull us in conflicting directions, just
as our relationships do. Anthropologists, like others, are "divided" selves
(Strathern 1988, 1999). We have one foot in the academy. The other in the
field. We are connected to our computer keyboards and notebooks even as
we exchange our experiences, insights, and stories with myriad other selves.
It is almost inevitable that, in our engagement with so many other selves, our
friends and interlocutors will fail to see eye to eye, just as our own analyses
might diverge from theirs. I was friends with both Marta and Roger when
in 2007 and 2008 I was completing my first of many field seasons to follow
in Nicaragua. The fact of my own political and ethical ambivalence was the
source of tremendous stress: anything I did to try to "give back" to one of
them was seen as a betrayal by the other. Yet, I eventually found that the
push and pull of those conflicting relationships, having become beholden to
both, was its own invaluable learning experience on my way to becoming
an anthropologist, not a scorpion. The ambivalence has since energized my
work, forced me to think about things from multiple perspectives, and even
helped me to develop new approaches to collaborative ethnography (see
Fisher and Nading, n.d.).

Anthropologists often seek ethical clarity in and from their work. Yet,
enmeshing ourselves in such complex and contradictory worlds—these fields

of relations that cannot help but generate ambiguity and ambivalence—is itself an integral part of the ethnographic process. Ethnography can be understood as a sort of ethical "worlding," a way of navigating and responding to a situation from within it (Chen, 2012). Moreover, in negotiating the various *aporia*—"non-passages" of social, political, and epistemological dilemma, in Spivak's (1999) terminology—we can start to come to terms with some uncomfortable truths about the colonial condition in which anthropologists continue to enmesh themselves. The key lesson—at once methodological, epistemological, and ethical—is not to swiftly dispatch those feelings of discomfort and ambivalence as impediments to doing ethnography. Rather, these positions are necessary for doing good ethnography. Anthropologists need to "stay with the trouble," as Haraway (2016) puts it, and allow these situations to produce new forms of understanding—of ourselves, of the world, and about how to give back.

ANIMAL METAPHORS AND SOCIAL CRITIQUES

In retrospect, I should have anticipated the issue of scorpionism. Animal metaphors are a common mode of social critique in Nicaragua. In the same year that I was chatting with Marta at the bus stop, local newspapers were littered with similar accusations in a public confrontation between municipal waste management employees, government employees, and a marginalized population of informal sector recyclers (called *churequeros*) during what was called *el churecazo*, or "the fiasco in La Chureca." These recyclers blockaded the unregulated, open-air dumps of both Ciudad Sandino and Managua. When municipal garbage trucks attempted to enter, trash-pickers pelted them with rocks. When police tried to drag them to jail, they set fire to makeshift barriers made of old car tires. They effectively halted the waste management infrastructure for several days, prompting a city-wide economic and public health crisis.

Recyclers' complaints were twofold: they were tired of seeing municipal garbage collectors, who already received government salaries for their work, cut into their economic bottom line by taking valuables out of the waste stream, selling them to intermediaries along their routes, and then dumping the remains. They were also upset about the increasingly marginalized status of their work. Sifting through waste for residual economic value is one thing. But when a Spanish magazine listed La Chureca as one of the "Twenty Horrors of the Modern World"—number three, to be precise, just ahead of the burning of the Amazon—La Chureca also became the focus of an international humanitarian crisis. "Like flies to dung" (*como moscas a mierda*), as one recycler put it, development organizations, Christian service groups, and brigades of poverty tourists were drawn to the site to bear witness to Nicaraguan poverty and to bring home with them photographic testimonials of injustice. Meanwhile, with the fallout of the churecazo, Nicaraguan politicians began to delegitimize recyclers' claims. They started referring to recyclers in public discourse as *zopilotes* (vultures) and compared their work to feeding off the detritus of society. The mayor of Managua at the time, Dionisio Marenco, even sympathized that trash-pickers might become so desperate as to consume the very same carrion birds that also inhabited their workplace. In a kind of political jiujitsu, recyclers attempted to wrest control of the narrative by characterizing themselves as *hormigas* (ants), a term which emphasizes the highly social, organized, and "grassroots" nature of their work. They also redirected blame to the class of *alacranes*, or scorpions, that tend to prey upon their labor, from the intermediaries that bought and sold the materials they collected to the municipal workers who extracted valuables before dumping the rest.

From this short vignette, it should be clear that, in Nicaragua at least, animal metaphors may serve as a kind of critical challenge. Animal symbolism itself has a long and storied history in the anthropological canon that illustrates the sheer richness of the arts of attention to the way things are (Brandes, 1984; Douglas, 1957; Leach, 1964; Tambiah, 1969). When animal metaphors are mobilized as a practice of politics, however, they instead refuse the way things are, and open up new terrains of struggle, if only by posing a situation in which things are other than what they seem. Hence, to call a human being a *zopilote*, or vulture, is to draw an unwanted comparison with a category of beings that feeds off the dead labor of society, and thus to interpellate a group of subjects as unwilling and unable to contribute to the livelihood of that society. To call oneself an *hormiga*, or ant, by contrast, is to emphasize one's disproportionate strength, work ethic, and propensity to cooperation and complex self-organization. To call someone else an *alacrán*, or scorpion—be they, in actuality, a humble municipal worker, a raw materials trader, a development worker, or an ethnographer—is to question their commitment to social life around them. If ideas are the flora and fauna of an "ecology of mind," as Bateson (1972) once wrote, the flora and fauna that co-populate human worlds—flies, vultures, ants, and scorpions—may also tell stories about the social worlds of human beings, though of course their particular "natures" constrain the kinds of stories that may be told about them.

Belonging to a class of eight-legged predatory arachnids, scorpions are distinguished by their grasping pedipalps (claws) and their narrow, segmented tail, which characteristically arches over their backs toward a venomous stinger, called a "telson." Some 2,000 species of scorpions are found on all continents, except Antarctica, where they have adapted to a wide range of environmental conditions, from deserts and jungles to prairies and the built environments of cities. In Nicaragua, scorpions promise painful encounters, but they are not deadly. A sting from a Nicaraguan scorpion is nothing that a strong pot of coffee won't cure, but as always, children, the elderly, and the infirm are most vulnerable. For Nicaraguans, it is the observed behavior of scorpions toward their own kin that is most troubling. When a scorpion mother gives birth to a "cyclone" of scorpions—arguably the most terrifying of all collective animal nouns in the English language—those tiny scorplings cluster on her back until they develop their hard carapace. Eventually, they will go their own way because scorpions are always and forever solitary hunters. In times of crisis, however, something curious happens: the mother does not sacrifice herself willingly, but the young scorplings will nevertheless converge back on their own mother, seize her, and cannibalize her for food.

"See?" Marta exhorted. "Scorpions are capitalists. They eat that which gives them life. Family. Friends. The earth. Whatever. That's what capitalists do."

LEARNING HOW TO GIVE BACK

If the problem of scorpionism in Nicaragua struck me as an interesting conceptual problem of "multispecies Marxism," to coin a phrase, it truly stung me as an ethnographer committed to ethical modes of engaging participants, doing research, and giving back. A significant part of my previous training as an anthropologist revolved around the inseparability of methods and ethics, and it tended to emphasize collaborative approaches to research design based on the premise that knowledge emerges *within* and *through* particular social relationships rather than by mere participation or observation. This primed me for my fieldwork in Nicaragua, where I was trying to understand how members of a pioneering clothing production chain—a Michigan-based ethical retailer called Clean Clothes Organics, a North Carolina–based NGO called CSD, and the members of two Nicaraguan cooperatives—negotiated very different understandings of "fair trade" (see Fisher 2013, 2016, 2018). I was unprepared, however, for the transformations effected by my own profound ambivalence regarding the whole matter.

This was, in a way, the opening that Marta saw in order to issue her warning early on in our friendship. I met Marta in the course of my first assignment in the field. Roger had been approached by a colleague from another NGO with the idea of staging an experimental employment-creation workshop in Nicaragua (See Fisher, 2010). The model, called *Laboratorio Organizacional del Terreno* (LOT, or the Organization Workshop in English), was developed by the close friend and prison cellmate of the legendary Brazilian teacher-scholar, Paulo Freire. Although LOT has been implemented around the world by entities as large as the International Labor Organization (ILO), this would be a historic first for Nicaragua. I accepted Roger's offer to serve as the technical director (*gerente técnico*), not because I thought I was qualified (I was not) or because I could contribute (I could not), but because I honestly thought it would benefit my fieldwork.

So, there I was, feeling completely out of my depth, managing the financial and logistical aspects of a month-long, city-wide workshop comprising several hundred unemployed and underemployed residents in Ciudad Sandino and two fledgling production cooperatives seeking organizational assistance. I found myself in a host of new situations, like walking around Mercado Oriental—Managua's sprawling, semi-formal central market—with more than 10,000 U.S. dollars in my pockets, flanked by a dozen leaders of these cooperatives. (Anyone familiar with Managua will note that under normal circumstances this would be unwise.) It was inevitable that I would make mistakes in my role. Thankfully, misplacing 10,000 dollars was not one of them. But the first misstep sincerely took me by surprise. As technical director, I decided to forego the stipend of 200 dollars allocated to the position. I thought myself quite generous because of it. But in so doing, I also made a big mistake: rather than accepting the stipend and *subsequently* donating it back to the cooperative as a gift, I refused it. My approach generated suspicion in several ways. First, what was I getting out of this arrangement that I did not need the 200 dollars? Second, among those who did not mistrust me but were instead skeptical of another faction in the cooperative, where did those funds eventually end up? A gift would have been a statement of reciprocity but unaccepted pay was unknown territory. Accepting the gift, moreover, would have allowed the workshop to make claims on me.

Although I created quite a mess, in the process I also made friends with Marta. She helped me negotiate conversations with these warring factions and provided me with a seemingly endless stream of gossip. When the workshop concluded, I started working earnestly with Génesis, the cotton-spinning cooperative that Marta helped found. They were in their very early stages, just working out the details of their constitution, which included governance protocols, while also starting construction on the building that would eventually become the cooperative's home. Part of the process of becoming a member entailed contributing to the construction effort five days a week, and so Marta and the others were there every workday contributing their "sweat equity." I thought at first that I could give back by working alongside them, which I did for almost a year. I helped dig a 2-meter-deep, 50-meter-long ditch that would become the building's foundation. I helped twist wrought iron rebar into frameworks that would serve as the bones of the building's concrete pillars. I helped lift heavy, concrete slabs, called *losetas*, to form the building's walls. In keeping with the ethnographic principle of participant observation, I performed this labor *with* and *alongside* my Nicaraguan colleagues, although I ultimately felt that I could make no pretense to understand the broader context of that labor—all the self-exploitation and significant social costs of doing that work, as they did, without immediate pay. As we chatted over lunch and went for beers at the day's end, I could not shake the feeling that I was getting something out of it *in the present tense*.

In February 2008, about midway through my first year in the field, my parents joined the millions of Americans who declare bankruptcy because of medical bills. For a bit of background, my mother and father live in the plains of Colorado. They are not poor, by their own accounting, but neither have they entertained the idea of retiring, least of all in their sixties. Rather, they live on a modest income that my mother brings in as a school bus driver and my father as a mid-level project manager at a technology and communications company. Both have worked every day of their adult lives, in some manner, and yet due to the nature of their health insurance plan at the time—the high-deductible, lifetime limit variety later prohibited by the Affordable Care Act in 2010—the precarity of their situation was cast into sharp relief.

I was in Nicaragua when it happened. I still remember the frail voice in which my father delivered the news of my mother's accident. It was the first time in my life I had ever heard his vulnerability, as if he were a shocked bystander trying to piece together for a police officer what had suddenly happened to his life. Furthest from my mind, at the time, was the economic repercussions that would resonate throughout my entire family, and that ended up being the real cost. Unable to pay a 50,000-dollar hospital bill, my parents declared bankruptcy. Shortly thereafter, just as I was completing my PhD and starting my first job in the throes of the Great Recession, the banks came after me. Because my father (and co-signer) had filed bankruptcy, my own student loans debts were considered to be in default—even though I had never missed a payment. (The ending to this particular story is beyond the scope of a chapter on debt itself, but suffice it to say the story is a good one: I march into the lenders' main offices, and I ultimately convince them to let me pay the debt through their boat insurance division.)

Still, the story pales in comparison to the broader lessons about the debts that anthropologists incur in the field. Marta helped me understand this, as well as the resiliency of human beings, which is far less a property of individuals than the social networks they have built to support them. As I told her, teary-eyed, about my parents, she told me about hers. Hers were farmers in the flatlands just east of Lake Managua. They lost their land, and all of their possessions, in 1968 when floodwaters overtook the doorway, then the roof. One of Marta's earliest memories is being carried in her mother's arms away from her home. In the early 1970s, her family was relocated to a pastureland just east of the capital city of Managua, a place then called OPEN-3 that would become Ciudad Sandino. There was no water. There were no roads. There were no shade trees, only the blistering sun. "It was hell," she says. "We were living in a ravine, trying to cook whatever food we could find over a campfire."

To say the least, I was chagrined by my own relativistic understanding of hardship. But once again, Marta and I made a connection because of our *different* experiences. "We're not different," she told me. "We've experienced different things, and that makes us different. You were born there, and I was born here, but we experience the same pain. What matters is that we're trying to help one another." No more than a few weeks later, I had the opportunity to rise to that challenge, make our relationship material. Marta's husband—a carpenter and furniture maker—had been released from a job with a wealthy patron in Managua and denied back wages for his work. Although I had no interest in becoming the patron in a patron-client relationship, I told Marta I wanted to help. "Sure," she told me, "that's what we call *solidaridad* [solidarity] or maybe *sociedad* [partnership]. It's something that poor people do to help one another, and you're a student so you still count [laughing]."

To help Marta, I commissioned a few pieces of furniture from her husband, all *abuelitas* (rocking chairs) which I knew from experience that tourists would appreciate. I fronted the money for the materials and labor and arranged the sale of those pieces to tourists I had met. The money was, thankfully, enough to get Marta and her family through to her husband's next job. I remember when she asked me one day about whether or not I wanted my share of the profits. "We're friends," I remember saying, proceeding to invent an aphorism that does not exactly exist: "There's no room for profit between friends." It was an awkward situation because in my own logic, I was rejecting the politics of exchange typically associated with patron-client relations, associated as they often are with scorpionism, but I also wanted to acknowledge our friendship, our solidarity, in the terms that this friendship actually existed: I did not need the money, but I knew something about the relative vulnerability of my friend and her family.

BROTHER TO A SCORPION, OR,
THE POSTCOLONIAL DILEMMA

In mid-2008, I started writing my dissertation. Following my fieldwork, I had hoped to stay in Nicaragua to write, and thus to disrupt the traditional separation between the keyboard and the field. But financial matters foreclosed on that option, and so I took the advice of my Nicaraguan friends—many of whom actually have personal if not also kin relations in the United States and receive remittances from them—and made the trip back to Oregon. There,

I learned firsthand about the phone calls that debtors make to family and friends, and the threatening, abusive, and demoralizing way in which they do it. My cell phone rang constantly. Each time it was someone trying to shame my parents and me, and to collect on "our" debts.

Meanwhile, I watched from afar the Génesis cooperative descend into chaos as the impact of the Great Recession reverberated through financial networks in New York all the way to Nicaragua. In 2008, CSD signed an agreement with a machinery trading company based in Charleston, South Carolina, called AAC. The company agreed to deliver a shipment of cotton- spinning and weaving machinery to Nicaragua for the Génesis cooperative on behalf of CSD, the primary financiers of the project, for approximately 400,000 dollars. The Carolinas are, of course, a historic site for clothing manufacturing in the United States, and so from a political- economic perspective it made sense that, as garment production jobs have made their way south over the past three decades, the material infrastructure would eventually follow. The year 2008, however, was a turbulent one for finances in the United States. The machinery trading company, allegedly under the direction of its own CEO, shipped rusted and broken machinery, having apparently gone to the effort of switching the metal serial number plates on the devices in order to pull off such a fraud. CSD tried to redress the issue on behalf of Génesis, but it was too late. The company had already gone under with the recession and filed for bankruptcy. CSD tried to sue them in court but was unsuccessful. It mobilized its activist network in the region to protest outside AAC's offices and the owner's own house, but again with no success. A law professor from Wake Forest University took up the case *pro bono* and attempted to prosecute the case under the RICO Act (the Racketeer Influenced and Corrupt Organizations Act), a statute usually applied to organized crime, but CSD ended up last in a very long line of plaintiffs who had suffered a similar fate. Five years later, CSD received a small fraction of what they lost as part of a settlement, but it was too little, too late for Génesis.

During this time, Marta's theory about Roger being a scorpion started to spread. Cooperative members suddenly had a litany of complaints. When they had appealed to him personally for support over the previous few years, they said that he had responded callously. When the deal fell apart, they claimed that he had obviously taken the money and run, leaving them with only a few thousand dollars each in return for their labor. He was dangerous, and members of the Génesis co-op would make that known to anyone who would listen. From Roger's perspective, by contrast, what he had done was eminently fair. As the director of a sustainable development NGO, his obligation was to the community, not to individuals, and so any support he offered took that form. As for their buy-out from the project, they received exactly the same amount they put in. As I have argued elsewhere (Fisher, 2013), the conflict had to do primarily with the different expectations these two groups brought to the project. For poor and working-class Nicaraguan cooperative members, "partnership" (*sociedad*) is not a matter of "fairness," in the Western liberal sense of the term, but a matter of social exchange in which both parties make claims on one another based on their particular relationships, and with the expectation that both parties will split the risks and reward equally. As for their labor, there is a fundamental contradiction between the way in which labor is experienced *en carne y hueso* ("in the flesh") over the course of five years, and the way it is subsequently counted and remunerated (i.e., as "sweat equity").

Try as they might, neither party could convince the other of their point of view. Roger brought in the lawyer from United States to deliver the news and explain the legal proceedings in person, though Génesis members were not convinced, because he could not speak Spanish and, as always, CSD performed the translation. For the first few years, the conflict was low-grade and found expression through lengthy meetings. All the while, cooperative members continued to come to work, without pay, in part because they believed things would work out, and in part because doing so gave them a sense of stability in their lives (Fisher, 2016). Eventually, that turned into all-out confrontation. Believing that it was CSD—not some North American machinery trading company—that had pocketed the money, as well as cooperative members' labor, Génesis forcibly took over the facility they had built. They called in support from the Sandinista Workers' Federation (CST), who successfully escalated the tension by hiring their own agents to fire mortars (the loud, explosive, homemade "firework" variety used in national celebrations) at CSD's offices. Members of Génesis, including Marta, also wrote me regular messages via Facebook and WhatsApp with the hope that I could help their cause against CSD. When I returned to Nicaragua in 2012, I met with Marta and apologized that I had been unable to help more, but that I didn't believe that CSD was their culprit. She smiled and laughed, and responded "Don't worry, you're still useful to us. You owe us, *doctor*."

I knew, of course, that CSD had not pocketed the money. I had been volunteering for CSD, raising money and working with their Nicaraguan projects *before* I even began to study anthropology. In that respect, my road to anthropology was somewhat heterodox because it ran through CSD, as I volunteered for them, and only later did Ciudad Sandino become my "field site." When I completed the research for my master's and PhD, I shared my conclusions with CSD and recommended certain changes in the way the NGO operated, and for doing so I was asked to serve on the organization's board of directors beginning in 2012. At the same time, because I had become a trusted friend of many members of the small NGO, they also asked me to serve as their check-writer for whatever business they conducted in the United States. In that role, I paid the bills for their quarterly newsletters and whatever other expenses they accrued in the process of collecting donations from their donor network in the United States. Every month, for three years, I also cut a check in the amount of just over 3,000 dollars to service the loan that CSD had taken out to purchase the machinery for the Génesis cooperative. When I started my first tenure-track job in North Carolina—not far from where CSD started out—I traveled with a network of CSD's supporters to protest outside of the offices of the company that had taken the NGO's money. I knew what Marta thought: CSD stole their labor, used their story to raise money they never saw, and preyed on poor and working-class Nicaraguan men and women. But I also knew what fate had befallen CSD's best intentions, and I was sympathetic to them, as well.

For five years, Génesis cooperative members went to work without pay, hoping that the situation would remedy itself. And for five years, I was caught in the middle of the slow-moving collision course between Génesis and CSD, both of whom counted me on their side. I felt committed to both of them: socially, ethically, and politically. No magical resolution came out of my conflicted role, only pain and suffering. And yet, for my part, I found new insight *because of* my sincere ambivalence about the whole thing. Indeed, this is one of the tremendous privileges of working as an anthropologist. What is a failure or even a catastrophe for others becomes an opportunity for important insight, in part because those situations create the conditions in which new kinds of interactions emerge that would otherwise be improbable in "everyday life."[4]

One must be very careful—and very conscientious—about how one uses that privilege, because one road leads to scorpionism. In my case, I found myself less inclined to think about why certain development projects "work" while others don't, and much more interested in how relationships are formed and play out across significant sociocultural and economic distance; how such projects are structured by formations of formal and informal knowledge; and how conflicts are not merely struggles for power and control but negotiations between (often equally legitimate) ethical positions. I became attuned to the ways in which transnational "partnerships" are laden with different ethical expectations for social exchange; how groups understand and "count" their labor; and how the daily practice of work figures into one's ethical self-fashioning. Along the way, my struggle to reconcile these two halves of my anthropological self led me to certain conclusions that I probably should have already reached: that a coloniality of knowledge characterizes all development projects (Escobar, 2018); that such projects are better understood as heterogeneous and indeterminate spaces of political-ethical negotiation (Gibson-Graham, 2006); and because anthropologists willingly and self-consciously entangle themselves in these situations, their obligations are not merely toward a project's "success," however defined, but rather are distributed across and throughout its many groups. The latter may sound like a daunting task, but that is also the point. In representing these complex situations through ethnography, we might adopt a kind of "cubist" perspective, as Auyero and Swistun (2009) describe it, in which one can see multiple sides of the story at the same time. So, too, in working out how to give back: negotiating these many conflicting ties of obligation is an integral part of an anthropologist's self-fashioning.

Two years after I met with Marta, in 2014, I was visiting Roger on the porch of his Ciudad Sandino home. We chatted about a number of things, and eventually the conversation turned to his earlier experiences training to become a Presbyterian minister in North Carolina, long before his work in Nicaragua started. Moving away from the church, he said, was an ethical decision principally because of the historical models provided by activist ministers in the American south. Roger was particularly inspired by the example of Reverend Will Campbell, a Baptist minister who had died about a year before. Campbell was the only founding member of the Southern Christian Leadership Conference, established by Dr. Martin Luther King, who was white. Campbell had famously rejected some of the political positions adopted by the Baptist church, declaring himself a "steeple dropout," a "bootleg preacher," and a "freelance civil rights activist"—all of which makes sense given his anti-institutional position that "church is a verb." Campbell used his moral position to protest the war in Vietnam, helping resisters find sanctuary in Canada. Although he kept his distance from political movements, he also saw racism in America as more than a political or legal problem of equal rights; in his view, it stemmed from a problem that had to do, above all, with the nature of humanity. And yet, he also believed that white nationalist, self-proclaimed Christian KKK members in upstate New York were, because of their beliefs, far more in need of his ministering than the black Muslims who once protected their own Grand Dragon.

Roger got up from his rocking chair, went to the bookshelf, and picked out a dusty paperback. "Here, read this," he said, as if it were the key to unlocking CSD's core ethic. Campbell's *Brother to a Dragonfly* (1977) is in part an autobiography of Campbell, his story of becoming a preacher and civil rights activist, escorting black students integrating the Little Rock public school system, and bearing witness to the founding of the Southern Christian Leadership Council. The book is also about his family, growing up in poor Amite County, Mississippi, and his love for and dedication to his older brother Joe, who became a pharmacist and developed a substance abuse problem that eventually took his life. As I read the book, I was somewhat confused by the message that Roger was trying to send: Was the theme of substance abuse in this narrative like capitalism to my friend? Did the dragonfly symbolize change, or self-actualization? Was this book about family trauma? I returned the book a few weeks later and posed my theories.

Roger turned to look at me, squinting with confusion, before a look of realization came over him: "Oh, right, I meant to give you this one." *Forty Acres and a Goat*, another autobiography published by Will Campbell, is the account of his friendship with a black man. For Roger, this book is a humbling recognition of the insurmountable differences between him and his friend—their life experiences and opportunities—because of their race. How, he asked, could they ever really come to know one another as friends? Campbell's solution is not to deny those inequalities, but to see them, to feel them, and then to work toward a world in which they are impossibilities. For Roger, that was nothing less than a spiritual problem: as Campbell himself put it, albeit in Roger's own paraphrasing, "One who understands the nature of God can never take sides."

CONCLUSION: A LIFE'S WORK

I did not think that Roger was a scorpion, but I understood why Marta did. As a general rule, people tend to fail at being scorpions, Roger included. They are generally aware of their debts, or else they are perfectly capable of making others aware of them (Cross, 2014). People also tend to care for those relationships from which those debts emerge. Ethnographic models such as the scorpion are thus not meant to indicate what a person is, but rather to act as a warning about what he or she could become. They are critical challenges, in word and deed.

I felt the sway of several kinds of debt in my fieldwork, as I felt the threat of dispatching those threats and becoming a scorpion. I felt a debt to my family and a call to care for my parents in their own moment of crisis. I felt the sting of those mathematically precise debts, driven by finance capital, that are generally detached from the human entanglements that animate particular lives (Graeber, 2009). And I felt the push and pull of the complex debts and reciprocities that are generated in ethnographic encounters, even as those inherited from family, finance, and friends simultaneously shaped how I ultimately came to understand what it means to be indebted.

My debts compelled me, in no small part, to tell this story in a way that captured what were not merely different but divergent perspectives. That was a challenge. More so when Génesis sued CSD in Nicaraguan courts in 2015 and then again in 2017. Co-op members asked me to intervene on their behalf by contributing my anthropological expertise, but I felt I could not do so because of my ties to CSD. The best I could do, I thought at the time, was to avoid casting blame—a classic relativist position. But my position was not one of free-floating, value-free objectivity. Admittedly, I made no judgment because I really never managed to arrive at a place of moral or political clarity regarding the whole matter.

Instead, my experiences of ambivalence and uncertainty taught me something else: the tremendous value of staying with the trouble. Working through these aporia—grappling with the "non-passages" produced by incommensurable experience—is, ironically, a way to see more clearly the postcolonial dilemma in which many anthropologists find themselves. It is a way of rethinking the complex and contradictory role that anthropologists play in development endeavors. And it is a way of developing a keener awareness of one's own political and ethical commitments as an anthropologist. Just as the "native anthropologist" is never fully *inside* or *outside* any given social context (Narayan, 1993), the many social ties that one develops in the process of practicing anthropology inevitably place the ethnographer betwixt and between. We are not "experts" because of our position as anthropologists; rather, we owe our expertise to the bundles of relations that make, and have made, our knowledge possible.[5]

I chose to highlight this complex nexus of debts here—debts inherited from parents, debts to capital interests, and those debts that we actively make as we self-consciously enmesh ourselves in plural fields of relations—because they speak to certain complexities about being an ethnographer that are not always honestly described, and because they are the origin of my own political and ethical commitments.

Recognizing one's debts is not sufficient. Working to pay them off is imperative. But even if those debts cannot be dispatched, it is still important to feel them, to allow oneself to be reminded of them, because that is how relationships are made and make us. We know what we know, and we are who we are, because of others. Taking account of and paying off one's debts is, therefore, not just methodological injunction, contributing to the project of "building rapport" as it is traditionally conceptualized. Building rapport is, instead, the precondition of any relationship we make, any debt we incur. And becoming an anthropologist is a debt that can never, really, be dispatched. It is a life's work.

NOTES

1. My gratitude to my interlocutors in Nicaragua, including Marta, Roger, members of the Gènesis and Fair Trade Zone cooperatives, and staff members at CSD, to whom I owe a great debt. Special thanks also to Michelle Johnson and Ned Searles, who nurtured the thoughts contained in this writing not only through their keen and insightful editing but ever since introducing me to cultural anthropology at Bucknell

University. I will always be your student! The material is based upon work supported by the National Science Foundation under Grant No. 1648667 and Doctoral Dissertation Improvement Grant No. 0753425.

2. The political structures that make ethnographic research possible are similar to the gendered divisions of labor that feminist political economists describe: certain activities are valued, counted, and ultimately remunerated, while others are devalued and made invisible (Hartsock 1983: 234; Gibson-Graham 1996; Waring 1988).

3. For Schensul et al. (1999:74, emphasis mine), "Building rapport means developing good personal relationships with people in the research setting *that facilitate access to activities and information necessary for conducting the study.*" Bernard (2011:277, citing Wolcott 2005) similarly remarks that "'Gaining rapport' is a euphemism for impression management, one of the 'darker arts' of field." In the subfield of economic anthropology, "negative reciprocity" is the term for treating social relationships as a means to the end of personal gain.

4. Jean Briggs (1970) recognized the value of failing to control her emotions, which in turn made possible her unique insights. This is similar to the insights of feminist philosophers of science, such as Isabelle Stengers who, along with Nobel Laureate Ilya Prigogine (Stengers and Prigogine 1984), demonstrate how divergences from normal conditions—in chemistry, nonequilibrium thermodynamics—reveal heretofore unseen properties of those involved.

5. Ten years later in 2016, that became the ethos of a collaborative, experimental workshop in Ciudad Sandino, entitled "A Political Ecology of Value" (Grant No. 1648667), which was funded by the National Science Foundation and developed with Alex Nading. With Isabelle Stengers, Anna Tsing, and others, we believe that finding oneself amid *different* positions—in this case, between different sectors of a city dealing with common problems—is what generates insight (Fisher and Nading n.d.).

Chapter 2

Predestined Help

Cosmology and Constraint in Transnational Fieldwork

Michelle C. Johnson

A HOLY MAN'S DREAM

I remember my first visit to Bafata-Oio, the Mandinga village in northern Guinea-Bissau where I conducted my first fieldwork in the late 1990s, as if it were yesterday even though it was over twenty years ago. Due to the challenges of travel in West Africa, my husband, Ned Searles—an Arctic anthropologist who had accompanied me for the year—my field assistant, Idrissa, and I arrived later than expected, around 8:00 p.m. Considering the time, I imagined an uneventful evening; maybe we would meet a few villagers before finding a place to sleep for the night. Instead, adults and seemingly endless groups of excited, curious children gathered to welcome us. The three wives of the village's renowned holy man, Al-Hajj Fodimaye Turé, who eventually became our adoptive father, cooked us a meal of *tiyaduurango* or, peanut sauce, a dish we later learned was only prepared on special occasions, such as life course rituals and Muslim holy days. After enjoying the delicious meal, we sat on woven mats under the light of the full moon, conversing with our hosts for hours before retiring to our private room furnished with a double straw mattress and a mosquito net, the most luxurious accommodation we had seen since our arrival in Guinea-Bissau six months previously. The next day, I introduced my research project to Al-Hajj and the council of elders and asked their permission to live and conduct fieldwork in the village. They agreed and even gifted my husband and me with a three-room mud-brick house at the edge of the village called "Kamarakunda" (to which we eventually added a cement floor and new thatch roof). We lived comfortably there for the remaining six months of my predoctoral fieldwork.[1]

19

I remember my husband and me asking each other, "Could entry into the field really be this easy?" I attempted to make sense of the situation. Perhaps it reflected comfortable West African attitudes toward strangers, as Gottlieb (2004) describes for the Beng people of Côte d'Ivoire. While Americans teach their children to fear and avoid strangers, the Beng, like other West African peoples, view them more positively; indeed, they welcome strangers as potential friends and allies. The Beng word for "stranger" is best translated into English as "visitor" or "guest," and strangers are "immediately incorporated into the local social universe." (Gottlieb 2004:149; see also Stoller and Olkes 1987:9 for a similar discussion for Songhay in Niger) This is also the case for the people of Bafata-Oio, who are distant linguistic relatives of the Beng, and who view strangers as auspicious, associating them with luck and opportunity. My interlocutors explained that strangers should be treated kindly because one never knows what position they might be in to help you in the future. As Mandinga are known historically for being great travelers, they explained: "You should treat strangers well because one day you might be one and you will expect the same treatment."[2]

Perhaps our warm welcome was also an expression of traditional Muslim hospitality, which Elizabeth Warnock Fernea describes so eloquently in her memoir, *Guests of the Sheik*. Always worrying that her household visits put a strain on her hosts' limited resources, Fernea (1989:44) commented: "Their traditional sense of hospitality always struggled with their slim budgets, and usually hospitality won." Muslim hospitality was a possibility, given that Mandinga are devout Muslims, who are looking increasingly beyond Africa for other models of being Muslim (Johnson, 2020).

But toward the end of my fieldwork, I learned of a different explanation: Karamadu, Al-Hajj's son and one of my most helpful research assistants, told us that several months before my husband and I arrived in the village, a holy man had a dream: two *tubaabulu*, or "white people," would arrive in the village and request to settle there. The holy man informed the villagers that when these people arrived, they should be treated with extra kindness since they will eventually do great things for the village. Karamadu explained that although the villagers were initially surprised that we were Americans rather than Arabs (Arab visitors were more common than Euro-American ones), everyone knew shortly after meeting us that we were the "white people" the dream had foretold—the ones to fulfill the prophecy.

In this chapter, I reflect on an anthropologist's predestined responsibility to "help" and how this fate contributed to efforts to compensate the people I worked with as I continued my research in Guinea-Bissau and later began a new related project with Guinean Muslim migrants in Portugal. I focus first on material forms of compensation and how these have been constrained by sociopolitical and economic realities in both sites, but especially in Guinea-Bissau. Finally, I consider the importance of non-material forms of compensation—specifically, return visits to the field and namesake relationships—as local forms of friendship and reciprocity. Considering the limitations of material gifts, I argue that non-material forms of compensation have been the most meaningful and enduring forms in my experience, so far. I contend that even though nonmaterial forms of compensation must never fully replace material forms, especially when the latter are desperately needed by people in the global south, they must be taken seriously as legitimate forms of compensation. First, however, it is necessary to say a bit about the places and people who inform this chapter.

MANDINGA IN GUINEA-BISSAU AND PORTUGAL

Guinea-Bissau is a lusophone, or Portuguese-speaking country in West Africa, located south of Senegal. Formerly known as Portuguese Guinea, it gained its independence from Portugal in 1974 after an eleven-year war of liberation led by revolutionary hero, Amílcar Cabral. It became the independent Republic of Guinea-Bissau in 1975. While Portuguese is the official language of the country, fewer than 10 percent of the country's 1.7 million inhabitants speak it, and they are concentrated in the capital city of Bissau. Kriolu—a blend of indigenous languages and Portuguese—is the country's *lingua franca* and is much more widely spoken, especially in the larger towns. There are also more than thirty different ethnic groups in Guinea-Bissau (Forrest 1992:118), many of which speak their own language. The Mandinga are the country's fourth largest ethnic group and make up about 15 percent of Guinea-Bissau's total population (Mendy and Lobban 2013:3).

Mandinga are part of the diaspora of Mande-speaking peoples in West Africa and trace their origin to the Mande heartland in present-day Mali. Because their origins lie elsewhere, members of Guinea-Bissau's indigenous coastal populations call Mandinga, along with other Muslim ethnic groups, such as the Fula and Beafada, "outsiders," even though they have been living in Guinea-Bissau for many centuries. Although Mandinga live in all parts of the country and form a relatively large population in the capital city, the majority still live in small towns and villages in the country's northern Oio region. Mandinga are Muslims, and practicing Islam is central to their personhood and identity. This further distinguishes them from Guinea-Bissau's coastal ethnic groups, who practice indigenous religions or Christianity or both. In this sense, Mandinga have more in common with other Muslim peoples in the neighboring countries of Guinea, Senegal, and Gambia than they do with Guinea-Bissau's indigenous peoples.

I conducted my fieldwork in the Mandinga village of Bafata-Oio, which at the time of my research had a population of approximately 900 people. The villagers make their living primarily as subsistence farmers. Women grow rice, millet, and maize for local consumption, and men grow peanuts and manioc as cash crops, which are sold in the nearby town of Farim or in Bissau, the capital city. Women also grow onions and distill salt from the brackish marshes located near the village, which they sell in Farim or at regional markets. They also harvest wild foods, such as oil palm nuts and baobab leaves, from the forest, and they hunt small game, such as guinea fowl and antelope, to supplement their diet. Although Mandinga do not consider themselves herders and often joke about their inferior skills in this area when compared to their Fula neighbors, some keep cattle, goats, and sheep, which are slaughtered for sacrifice during life course rituals and on Muslim holy days.

Although at first glance Bafata-Oio appears to be a typical Mandinga village, it is actually a renowned pilgrimage site to which visitors from several West African and European countries travel to attend Gammo, the Prophet's Birthday festival. Once a year, thousands of pilgrims descend on the village for this three-day festival to feast, chant verses from the Qur'an, and seek blessings from Al-Hajj Fodimaye Turé, a renowned Muslim healer-diviner. After Al-Hajj's death in 2008, pilgrims still make the journey to Bafata-Oio yearly to visit his grave, seeking luck and blessings from a now powerful ancestor (Johnson 2014:42). Bafata-Oio's status as a regional pilgrimage site, as well as its relative proximity (a forty-five-minute walk and short canoe ride across the Farim River) to the town of Farim gives the village a relatively cosmopolitan feel, rendering it "remotely global." (Piot 1999) During my fieldwork, I spent my days working with women in the rice fields, at the salt flats, and in their daily routines of cooking and caring for children. I attended many life course events, such as name-giving rituals, weddings, and funerals; my first research project focused on girls' initiation rituals and local responses to the global debate over female circumcision (see Johnson, 2000).

As I was preparing for a second year of fieldwork in 1998, a coup prompted an eleven-month civil war—known locally as the War of June 7th—and prevented me from returning to Guinea-Bissau. Determined to continue my research, I sought advice from my professors and friends. A fellow anthropologist and friend who worked with Sierra Leonean immigrants in Washington, DC after a civil war prevented her from returning to Sierra Leone (see D'Alisera, 2004), encouraged me to conduct my fieldwork in Portugal. In 1999, I spent one year in Lisbon researching the religious lives of Guinean Muslim (ethnically Mandinga and Fula) immigrants and refugees, who were pouring into the city as a result of the war. Migration from Guinea-Bissau to Portugal began in the 1950s with an elite group of migrants of mixed

Portuguese and African descent who sought educational opportunities in Europe (Carvalho 2012:19–20). Guinea-Bissau's independence in 1974 initiated a larger wave of immigration. The Guinean Muslim migrants I worked with in Lisbon, however, were part of the largest wave of immigration to Portugal, which occurred in the 1980s and 1990s (Machado, 1998).

The migrants I came to know lived in apartments in central Lisbon or in the city's many exurbs, some of which were inhabited almost entirely by African immigrants from Portugal's former African colonies, Guinea-Bissau, Cape Verde, Angola, Mozambique, and São Tomé. Many of the younger men worked in construction while the older men made their living as Muslim healer-diviners, helping their clients with a variety of problems, from business pursuits to drug addiction. Others sold food and other products from the homeland such as palm oil, okra, local tobacco, and kola nuts on the streets in central Lisbon or in shops in the various exurbs (see Johnson, 2016). Many women sold clothing or cleaned offices and private homes. Others owned or worked in Guinean restaurants or assisted their healer-diviner husbands by booking appointments or translating for clients who did not speak Mandinga, Fula, or Kriolu. During my fieldwork, I visited members of the migrant community in their homes, in restaurants and work places, and at Lisbon's central mosque. I also joined the Maternal Kin Club, a prominent Mandinga women's association in Lisbon, and attended life course rituals and Muslim holy days, which brought members of the dispersed community together. My transnational fieldwork was fascinating because I had the opportunity to work with people in Portugal whom I had previously known in Guinea-Bissau, as well as to travel back to Guinea-Bissau with several research participants from Lisbon. These experiences deepened my understanding of both field-sites and the complex relationship between them. It also doubled my "informant pool" and made me accountable (and indebted) to multiple communities on and between two interconnected continents.

PREDESTINED HELP? COMPENSATION AND COSMOLOGY

While anthropologists have always had to consider how to compensate their hosts for their time and knowledge, the issue of compensation in fieldwork only emerged as a topic of formal anthropological inquiry in the 1990s. In an attempt to cultivate more scholarly attention on the issue for the journal *Anthropology Today*, Kingston, Gottlieb, and Benthall (1997:27) asked: "What form of exchange to communities, individuals, and families is appropriate for the provision of information and hospitality?" Specifically, they were interested in what form compensation should take (i.e., money or gifts in kind), as well as more sustained forms of reciprocity that extends beyond anthropologists' initial fieldwork. Gottlieb and Graham (1999) discussed issues of ongoing reciprocity and relationship with the communities they featured in their first co-authored memoir, *Parallel Worlds* (1993), and after, their use of the royalties they earned from the sale of the book to fund several small-scale development projects in two Beng villages in Cote d'Ivoire (2012). Their decision was consistent with the professional stance that regards immediate or short-lived compensation as insufficient: "A far more active, even lifelong commitment to our field communities is morally required" (Gottlieb and Graham 1999:118; cf. Pink 1998).[3]

Today, as Institutional Review Boards become more formalized and rigorous, researchers are encouraged, even expected, more than ever to reflect seriously on the benefits of their proposed projects to "research subjects." Compensation has thus become an issue not just for anthropologists, but for institutions and granting organizations to consider, as well. Students of anthropology are also beginning to tackle this issue earlier. While some learn about it for the first time in graduate school, college students today often take up the issue in methods courses, which are increasingly more common at the undergraduate level. At the university where I teach, anthropology majors are required to take such a course. We devote several classes to research ethics and require the students to complete the IRB training modules and submit their research proposals for a mock review (at Bucknell, research conducted for courses and not intended for publication is exempt from the formal review process).

When I submitted my first IRB proposal as a graduate student at the University of Illinois, ethnographic research was exempt from the full review process, and I was forced to think very little about the quality of my relationship with members of the local communities with whom I would work, including how to appropriately compensate them for their hospitality, time, and stories—in short, for their willingness to let me (and my husband) into their lives. In the early days of my fieldwork in Guinea-Bissau, before I knew of the holy man's dream, this issue resolved itself as we "lived together," as our Mandinga hosts put it, and became entangled in a web of community. Unlike in the eastern Canadian Arctic, where I had accompanied my husband for his fieldwork two years previously, Mandinga did not consider money a culturally appropriate form of compensation, and paying our hosts for their time or knowledge would have insulted them. On the rare occasions when money was appropriate—such as visits to elders or healer-diviners, or in the case that someone had a very specific need for cash—we had to conceal the cash underneath a more visibly prominent gift in kind, such as sugar, salt, candles, or kola nuts, which served to "purify" it. My Guinean Muslims interlocutors in both fieldsites were well aware of money's ability to alienate and corrupt, as evidenced by the common Kriolu phrase, *kume dinheru* (to "eat money"), which people in power were described as doing regularly and voraciously at the expense of the poor and powerless.[4]

Mandinga considered gifts morally superior to money and thus valued them more. I also found that opportunities to present gifts were ubiquitous during my fieldwork in both Guinea-Bissau and Portugal. For example, one woman in Bafata-Oio, Saajo, filled our *puti*, or water storage pot, with potable water from the village pump twice weekly. We appreciated this since neither my husband nor I could carry water that far without spilling it and I never learned to balance heavy loads on my head as Mandinga children and adults so expertly did. To show our appreciation for Saajo's efforts, we gave her a sack of imported rice to supplement her own crop.

We learned the contours of the local gift economy through trial and error: what to give, and how and when to give it. On one occasion when I was quick to return a hoe shortly after I borrowed it, I expected the neighbor who loaned me it to be pleased by my efficiency in returning it. Instead, he seemed disappointed. When I discussed this with my research assistant, he explained that my neighbor had interpreted my prompt return of his hoe as an indicator of my lack of interest in being his friend. Delaying verbal expressions of gratitude and the presentations of gifts (including returning borrowed objects) create and sustain friendship.[5] Our Mandinga hosts delighted in our efforts to understand and follow those and other rules of reciprocity. Occasionally, people would remind us of the primacy of friendship over gifts by politely declining the latter, saying "In the name of God [which one must say when politely declining something], Fatumata, just build my name in America," which was really their way of saying, "Don't forget me after you leave."

Considering the relative ease with which we learned how to appropriately compensate our hosts, I was a bit taken aback by the holy man's dream, as it raised questions I still struggle to answer today. I confess I still ponder the taboo question for anthropologists of religion (forgive me, Evans-Pritchard): Did the holy man *really* have that dream, or was this simply the villagers' way of understanding our presence and solidifying our belonging? Why, after all, would a foreign couple come all the way from America, braving the heat and mosquitoes just to learn about their culture? Considering that both Mandinga "custom" (*aadoo*) and Islamic codes of hospitality prevented our hosts from demanding money for the time and knowledge they imparted us, perhaps the dream was a culturally acceptable way of ensuring that the visitors would give them something in return beyond kola nuts, friendship, and the chance to have their name "heard" in America. Maybe this expectation had always been there, albeit never made explicit, and in my own naiveté as a young fieldworker, I had simply missed it. But in attempting to understand this myself, I return to Evans-Pritchard's (1937) study of Azande witchcraft:

whether or not the old man's dream—like witches for Azande—was "true" or not is irrelevant: the dream, real or fashioned, shaped both initial encounter and ongoing relationship between anthropologists and hosts. In this sense, it was real enough to be taken seriously.

If the dream shaped the ongoing relationship between the visiting anthropologists and the local people, it also put considerable pressure on us. The expectation that my husband and I would one day do "great things" for the village was hard enough to swallow, but the idea that our very presence and the great things we would allegedly do were divinely inspired (Muslim holy men are believed to receive messages from God via angels) made us uncomfortable, to say the least. My thoughts went immediately to Paul Stoller's account of his apprenticeship with a Songhay sorcerer during his fieldwork in the Republic of Niger. On one occasion, a bird shat on his head, which Stoller's friend interpreted as a "sign" that Stoller should become his apprentice and learn to be a *sorko* (Stoller 1989:40–1; see also, Stoller and Olkes, 1987). At first, Stoller admits that he had a difficult time writing about this and other "supernatural" events that he experienced in the field because they challenged the conventions of "ethnographic realism" (Stoller 1989:47).

My own worry, in contrast, was more mundane and practical in nature: What if we failed to fulfill the prophecy? My husband and I were both in an early, uncertain period in our graduate education: Would we ever finish our dissertations? That was only the beginning of our concerns. Given an increasingly competitive job market, would we manage to obtain academic positions at all, let alone in the same university or town? Would we have children and learn to juggle our double academic careers and parenthood? These concerns were difficult, if not impossible, for our Mandinga hosts to imagine, especially since they viewed all "white people" as having unlimited access to both opportunities and cash (see Pink, 1998). From their perspective, we should have no trouble meeting the expectations set by the dream; given our lot in life, how could we be destined for anything less than success?

This characterization of Ned and me as being destined for success was very common during my fieldwork. On one occasion in Bissau's Bandé Market, for example, I joined a group of Mandinga men for lunch. One man asked me if I could get him a visa so he could go to America. He had seen pictures of people getting money from machines, he explained, and he wanted to do this, as well. I attempted to explain that this was not exactly how it appeared, that people had to first put money in their bank accounts before they could withdraw it. I also challenged him on his assumptions about America, informing him about the realities of racism and poverty. I explained that many people in the United States lacked money to buy food and medicine and had to live on the streets. Unlike in Guinea-Bissau, where it is customary for people to invite strangers to eat with them, I continued, in America most people simply ignore the hungry. But the man did not find my stories convincing and accused me of telling him "lies" in order to prevent him and other Guineans from migrating.

Two years later, I met this man on the streets of Lisbon. We recognized each other immediately. After exchanging greetings, he told me that I was right about what I had told him in Bissau and that he should have listened to me more carefully: "Life in *Tubaabuduu* (the 'place of the white people'— Mandinga often conflate Europe and North America) is hard," he confessed, and he told me that he was planning on returning to Guinea-Bissau.

Issues of compensation were similar in some respects in Lisbon and profoundly different in others. My interlocutors in Lisbon were on the whole more affluent than their West African counterparts. Although many complained that they had little money to send back to Guinea-Bissau in the form of remittances, they marveled at how much easier life was in Europe. Food was easier to obtain, for example, and staples, such as rice, oil, and meat, were considerably more affordable in Lisbon than back home. Most female migrants I worked with were not as mobile as I was, however, so when I visited them in the suburbs, I often brought them "things from the homeland," such as vegetables, local tobacco, and kola nuts, which I purchased from the Guinean merchants at Rossio in central Lisbon. Women appreciated these gifts (cf. Gottlieb, 2012a), which had the dual function of enhancing the flavor of local dishes and engaging their memory about life back home: the beauty of the land, the freshness of the food, and the "sweetness" of life in Africa when compared to the stress, racism, and Islamophobia of Europe.

Some items, like kola nuts, were more difficult to obtain and were considerably more expensive in Lisbon than in Guinea-Bissau. Because of this, they were often absent at life course rituals, even when they were supposed to play a central role. When I asked one man how a baby can receive a name without kola nuts to share with guests, he just shrugged his shoulders and said, "It can't be helped, Fatumata, life in Europe is different." Whenever I could, I volunteered to provide the kola nuts for ritual events, which delighted my hosts. On other occasions when women lacked money to travel to a ritual or buy credit for their mobile phones, I would pay their fares or lend them my phone to make calls (see Johnson, 2013). When people had difficulty with immigration papers, I assisted them. In fact, during my 1999 fieldwork in Lisbon, I experienced my own difficulty obtaining my research visa and had to spend several hours a day for a week at a time, standing in line at Lisbon's *Serviços de Estrangeiros e Fronteiras* ("Foreigners and Borders Service"). As I waited, I helped immigrants from Guinea-Bissau and Cape Verde fill out the forms, as many of them could not read or write Portuguese. I also met several people there who later shared their life stories with me and thus helped me with my research.

In Lisbon, I also gave many more monetary gifts. Although people had more money, they were also more dependent on money, had more needs and wants that required cash, and felt considerable pressure to send remittances to their relatives back home. After Portugal joined the European Union and the euro replaced the escudo, many people, Portuguese and Guineans alike, complained their money did not stretch as it used to. As in Guinea-Bissau, however, immigrants refused to be paid cash alone for interviews, so whenever I gave money, I always presented it under kola nuts, local tobacco, or a bag of okra from Guinea-Bissau, to "purify" it.[6]

"LIVING TOGETHER" OVER TIME: COMPENSATION AND CONSTRAINT

Compensation, however, is about more than merely paying one's hosts for their time and knowledge; it is about negotiating changing relationships and "living together" over time. As my husband and I prepared to leave Bafata-Oio after my first fieldwork, we pondered this challenge carefully. Shortly before returning, we presented a *semola* ("offering" or "sacrifice") to the entire village: a farewell meal consisting of cooked rice and goat meat garnished with a sauce made from vegetable oil, tomato paste, bitter tomatoes, and hot pepper. After the meal, we announced an additional gift, one we

Figure 2.1   The Village Mosque Pre-Renovation, 1997.

imagined might more closely meet the expectations set by the holy man's dream: we would use my remaining grant money to purchase supplies to renovate the crumbling village mosque. We would pay for new mud bricks, white paint, and, most importantly, a corrugated tin roof (see Figures 2.1 and 2.2). We also made a promise. While the villagers were very proud of their annual Prophet's Birthday festival, they claimed that it lacked one thing: light. My husband and I vowed that one day, God willing, we would return to the village with a gas-powered generator to light up the festival.

Six years later, in 2003, Ned and I returned to Guinea-Bissau. A lot had happened during our absence. I had completed a year of fieldwork in Lisbon and had later returned there twice for follow-up research. My husband and I both finished our dissertations and obtained our doctoral degrees. Our entry into the job market had been fruitful: In 2002, we accepted positions at Bucknell University and I used my start-up research funds to finance my 2003 return to Guinea-Bissau and Portugal.

In Guinea-Bissau, we spent the first week of our stay in Sintra, the neighborhood in Bissau where we had lived before. Old friends were delighted by our return and shared stories about the recent civil war and updated us on who had died, who had fled, and who was still alive and well in Bissau. Excited to return to the village, we bought a generator at a store downtown and boarded a bush taxi headed north. We arrived at the entrance to the road to the village in a torrential downpour. We worried how we would

Figure 2.2   The Village Mosque Post-Renovation, 2000. Photograph by Joanna Davidson.

get our belongings, especially the generator, to Bafata-Oio, a 45-minute walk through the salt marshes. No donkey carts were operating because of the heavy rain, so we begged the driver to brave the roads and take us all the way into the village; reluctantly, and for a hefty fee, he agreed. Our return was everything an anthropologist could dream of (see Bruner, 1999): groups of soaking-wet children cheered and waved as the bush taxi stopped in the place our house once stood (we were prepared for the shock, since we had received news that it had collapsed during the civil war). Al-Hajj and the villagers were as delighted to see us as we were to see them. Although they were disappointed to see that we (still) had no children in tow, the generator seemed to make up for it, at least in the short term: we had, after six years, fulfilled our promise. We later learned, however, that Al-Hajj and the elders had hoped for a much larger generator: the one we

Figure 2.3   Setting Up the Generator, 2003.

brought would only power a few light bulbs, not nearly enough to light up the entire village for the Prophet's Birthday festival. As we shopped for a generator, we were shocked to find that even the smallest one cost three times what we had expected (as the research trip alone exhausted my modest start-up grant, the generator was an out-of-pocket expense). We also worried that a larger generator would be difficult to transport to the village, given that we did not have our own car and had to rely on public transportation (see Figure 2.3).

Although I have not returned to Guinea-Bissau since 2003, I still feel the obligation to continue giving to the people who made me an anthropologist and without whom I would have never been able to work in Portugal (cf. Pink, 1998). As I have pondered over the years what forms such giving might take, I have had some very good examples. My graduate school mentor and her husband donated the royalties from their jointly authored, *Parallel Worlds* (Gottlieb and Graham, 1993), to the two Beng villages in which they lived and worked in Côte d'Ivoire (Gottlieb and Graham 1999:119). They also provided a new water pump, fifty plastic chairs, and a stereo system, at their hosts' request (see Gottlieb and Graham 2012:91). Most impressively, they brought Bertin, one of Alma's most gifted research assistants, to the United States and sponsored him as he pursued a degree at the University of Illinois, where they both taught. As a young graduate student, I marveled at these efforts and pledged to do similar things for "my people" in Guinea-Bissau.[7]

When Ned and I were in the position to make similar contributions, I encountered seemingly insurmountable logistics. Guinea-Bissau's 1998 civil war and resulting political instability—the country has been deemed the "world's first 'narco-state'" (Chabal and Green 2016:1)—rendered return to the country and even communication with our Mandinga hosts difficult, even impossible at times, despite the promise of technology to render the world a hyper-connected, global village (see Ferguson, 2006). We had to find other ways of maintaining ties with the village. Numoo, Al-Hajj's son and one of my most beloved research assistants, dreamed of pursuing an education abroad. While he had always imagined Portugal as an obvious destination, after meeting and working with my husband and me in Bafata-Oio, he wanted to go to the United States instead. But as much as my husband and I liked this plan, we knew that it was, unfortunately, unrealistic. At the time of my fieldwork, Guinea-Bissau had no university and only one scholarly institute, the Instituto Nacional de Estudos e Pesquisa (National Institute for Study and Research). The country's elementary school system was also one of the poorest in Africa (see Forrest, 1992).[8] Despite Numoo's intellectual curiosity, he had only a few years of formal education beyond the village Qur'anic school, was only moderately literate in Portuguese (his Kriolu, however, was exceptional), and spoke only a word or two of English. But this was only part of the problem. Even if he managed to secure a visa and learn English, where would he pursue his degree? Bucknell is a selective liberal arts university that serves primarily white, middle-class suburban students, many of whom attended elite boarding schools. The cost of attendance is approximately $70,000 a year. Even with two full-time faculty salaries, my husband and I were still untenured at the time, and there was no way we could afford to sponsor Numoo, even if he received a scholarship and/or financial aid. So, we compromised: Numoo's Arabic was better than his Portuguese, so he applied to the University of Blida in Algeria, was accepted, and received a partial scholarship. We paid his remaining tuition and living expenses, which were well within our budget. We also gave him money to buy a laptop computer to aid him in his studies and even managed to send him back to Bafata-Oio once a year to visit his family and attend the Prophet's Birthday festival. After graduating from university, Numoo returned to Guinea-Bissau where he received a prestigious government job in Bissau. My husband and I delighted that we had a hand in his success, and Numoo assured us that even though we were unable to return to the village ourselves, he was living proof that we had not forgotten them.

THE POWER OF NONMATERIAL FORMS OF COMPENSATION: RETURN AND NAMESAKES

Our material efforts to give back to our Mandinga hosts have never felt adequate, and perhaps they never will, considering that I now face the challenges of managing two fieldsites and the multiple layers of relationship and indebtedness that come with transnational research. I have, perhaps, fared better in the realm of the nonmaterial. Our 2003 return to the village was especially meaningful to both us and our Mandinga hosts. In their coedited volume, *Returns to the Field*, Howell and Talle take up the practice of "multitemporal fieldwork," which they define as "many returns to the same place across the years, but not necessarily in a systematic chronological pattern." (2012a:3) Although they acknowledge that most anthropologists return to their fieldsites, very few have discussed the methodological and analytical implications of this common practice. They argue (2012a:3), "Multitemporal fieldwork enhances our knowledge in many ways: about the people we study, about patterns of social and cultural life, about ourselves, and about the central tenets of anthropological theory."

Wolcott (2008:61) once wrote that leaving the field and returning as promised often results in a "strengthening of relationships" between fieldworkers and their communities. This strengthening is evident in Bruner's discussion of his return to Sumatra, four decades after his initial fieldwork. Although the real purpose of his article is to underscore how Indonesia, anthropology, and the world have changed over the course of four decades, the power of return is clear: Bruner and his family were warmly received by the Toba Batak people, all of whom either remembered them or had, at the very least, heard stories about them. A ritual was held in their honor, which included singing, dancing, ritual speeches, and the presentation of gifts, including money and sacred cloth. People told stories, many of which the Bruners themselves had long forgotten (Bruner 1999:466–7).

Such stories of return underscore the importance of relationship and memory in anthropological encounters. In my own case, communication—in the form of letters, mobile phone conversations, email and WhatsApp messages, and sending money through Western Union—and return visits to both field-sites were important for anthropologists and hosts alike. Forgetting, people often told us, is easy to do; our efforts demonstrated that, despite the passage of time, we had not forgotten our hosts. Communication and return visits were even more powerful and meaningful given that they happened despite challenging obstacles, including a civil war and persistent political instability.

Beyond return, *toomaa*, or namesake relationships, are another powerful—and even more enduring—form of non-material reciprocity. Naming practices and their cultural significance remain understudied in anthropology (see vom Bruck and Bodenhorn, 2006), a surprising fact given that anthropologists are commonly "adopted" by the people they work with and receive local names. Miller (2001:154) writes, "Naming is foremost a recognition of common humanity and kinship." Names are very important among Mandinga and other peoples in West Africa, and individuals have multiple names. A family name, inherited from one's father, provides a person with a clan affiliation, and members of a single clan are imagined as related to one other, even if they are not close "blood" relatives. Clan names also position people in society, providing members with a totem (though not everyone today actually remembers their totem) and structure relationships with other clan members, such as "joking cousin" (*sanawoo*) relationships. Joking cousins ritually insult one another during greetings, take freely from one another in times of need or just for fun, and intervene on each other's behalf in times of conflict. It is taboo for a person to harm a joking cousin. Aside from clan names, people have given names, which are usually Muslim names that people receive on the day of their name-giving ritual, which takes place seven days after birth (Johnson 2017, 2020). People who have the same given name are called *toomaa*, or "namesake," and have an especially close relationship. They are believed to share seven personality traits, which are said to flow directly between their bodies. Over the years in Guinea-Bissau and Portugal, my husband and I have both become enmeshed in several *toomaa* relationships, as have our children, who accompanied us to Lisbon for my 2011 fieldwork. During my first fieldwork in Guinea-Bissau, Saajo gave her newborn daughter my Mandinga/Muslim given name, Fatumata. I soon learned, however, that this was not just an ordinary namesake; it was a *bonotoo*, or "loser name": Saajo had given birth previously to seven daughters, all of whom had died as infants or young children. People believed that her excessive misfortune was due to an *iran* spirit that was "stuck behind" her. Unable to have children of its own, the *iran* had resorted, as *iran* often does, to "taking" human infants or young children, in this case, all of Saajo's daughters, hitting them on the backs of their necks with an invisible machete and ending their lives in a single blow. When Saajo became pregnant again, she sought treatment in the form of amulets and prayers for a boy. But despite her efforts, she gave birth to another girl, my namesake, whom people called "White Fatumata." "Iran may be powerful," people asserted, "but they are no match for white people."

Naming an ill-fated infant after a foreigner—someone associated with power and opportunity, and whom *iran* are more prone to leave alone—was, according to our hosts, a good way to attempt to alter the little one's fate. My husband was also implicated in the relationship. Since White Fatumata shared his own wife's name, he was expected to treat her as such. He called her "my wife" and gave her money, food, clothing, and shoes. In the end, this strategy worked: when we returned to the village in 2003, White Fatumata was seven years old. People claimed that she shared many of my traits: she feared the hot sun and preferred Qur'anic study over farming. In 2008 when I received a phone call from Numoo's older brother, Karamadu, I inquired about my namesake. He told me that she was well and that the elders had made an exception, allowing White Fatumata to attend Qur'anic school with the boys, whom she was outperforming. Karamadu laughed: "It's not her fault, Fatumata; she's your namesake" (see Figure 2.4).

Our Mandinga hosts in Guinea-Bissau and Portugal alike were delighted when my husband and I (finally) became parents and gave our children both American and Mandinga names. We named them Al-Hajj and Aja, after Al-Hajj Fodimaye Turé, Bafata-Oio's former holy man and our "father," and his first wife, who was the first woman in the village to make the Hajj, or pilgrimage to Mecca. During my 2011 fieldwork in Lisbon, I learned that one of my closest research participants and friends, Bacar, died suddenly from an illness. His wife, Aminata, had remarried and she and her husband had a daughter, whom they named Fatumata, my first namesake in Lisbon. Shortly after my son, "Al-Hajj" turned seven years old, he became interested in the Arabic language. One day at a bookstore in our town, he picked out an Arabic phrase book and studied it every morning on the bus ride to and from school. He also began asking my husband and me about the Qur'an, which we had studied with a teacher in Lisbon, and he asked if we would teach him what we know.

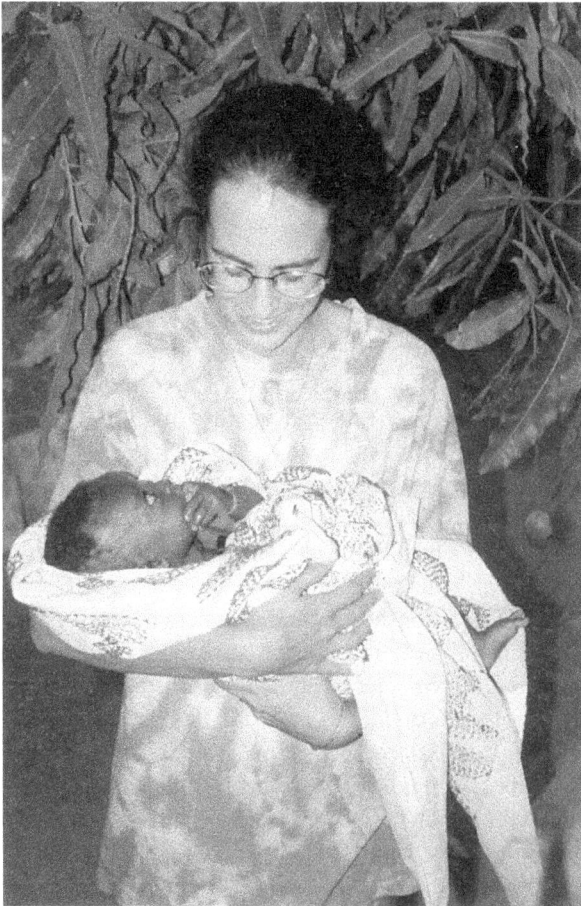

Figure 2.4   The Author with "White Fatumata," 1997. Photograph by Ned Searles.

We taught him the first few *suras*, which he memorized quickly. He wanted to learn more, so with his allowance money he purchased a Qur'anic recitation application on his iPad. When I returned to Lisbon for my 2017 fieldwork, I shared these stories, as well as a video I took of "Al-Hajj," chanting the Qur'an (he had actually gotten quite good), with members of the Guinean Muslim community in Lisbon. While our son's passion for Islam amazed my husband and me—especially since we had done nothing to encourage him beyond simply explaining how he got his name—my interlocutors in Lisbon did not find it surprising at all: what else would one expect from someone who was named after a renowned Muslim holy man?[9]

A few years ago, my husband and I received an email from Numoo, informing us that he had married and had two children, a boy and a girl, whom he and his wife named Lamini and Fatumata (our Mandinga names), but whom they called Ned and Michelle (our American names). For Mandinga, namesakes are enduring symbols of deep, mutual relationship. Money often gets lost or stolen, mud bricks collapse, and paint fades over time, but names outlast them all: transcending distance and even death, they prevent people from forgetting, even when distance complicates face-to-face relationships.

FATIMA'S DREAM

Reciprocity between anthropologists and their interlocutors is never-ending and dynamic. Compensation—how and what anthropologists give back to research participants for their time, hospitality, and knowledge—is difficult to negotiate, and expectations change over time. In both Guinea-Bissau and Portugal, noncash gifts are more appropriate than cash, but I have demonstrated the difficulty of navigating the logistics of such gift-giving, considering political conflict, the digital divide and other structural inequalities, religious and cultural beliefs surrounding "helping," and transnational fieldwork, which extends relationship and indebtedness beyond a single fieldsite.[10]

When material forms of compensation are culturally inappropriate or not feasible, non-material forms can be powerful substitutes. I have considered two such forms: return visits to the field and namesake relationships. These two forms of non-material compensation ground the relationship between anthropologists and their hosts in dynamic, enduring human relationship. Given the effectiveness of these nonmaterial forms, as well as the cultural value and meanings they have for local people, they must be considered legitimate forms of compensation. Beyond being durable and easily attainable, even in the worst of situations, they remind us of anthropology's most important gifts, which have become even more important—even priceless—given our own country's political climate and the state of the world today: cultural understanding and friendship rooted in our common humanity.

I do not believe, however, that nonmaterial forms of compensation should replace material forms, especially when the latter are possible, easily obtained, and desperately needed to improve people' lives in the communities where anthropologists work. Perhaps the best practice is for both forms to coexist. As the political situation in Guinea-Bissau has improved and Guineans in Lisbon begin to visit home more frequently, opportunities for non-material forms of compensation are beginning to present themselves. These are especially powerful when they come not from the anthropologist, but from the local people themselves. Even better, as Pink (1998:11) argues, the current model—in which anthropologists feel obligated to compensate local people for what they take—should be replaced by a more collaborative one, "the idea of anthropologist and informant 'creating something together'." This model, she contends, gives agency to both parties, rather than just to the anthropologist. But it also demands that the people with whom anthropologists work have more material resources and more cultural capital than they often have in today's world, which is plagued by worsening inequalities.

In my own case, I experienced the possibility for a more collaborative compensatory project for the first time during my 2017 fieldwork. One morning, I traveled to Carnexide, a 45-minute bus ride from central Lisbon, to spend the day with Mansata and Al-Hajj, a Mandinga couple I have known since 1999. We cooked "food from the homeland" together, reminisced about the past, and updated each other on our lives. Their daughter, Fatima, whom I interviewed extensively during my first fieldwork in Lisbon, had migrated to England where she married and had three children. Excited, I told Mansata how much I missed seeing her. Mansata went to her bedroom and returned with her mobile phone and a pair of headphones. She called Fatima in England through WhatsApp, and we talked for an hour. She told me about her children, about what daily life is like in England for her as a Muslim woman, and about her most recent trip to Guinea-Bissau. Fatima told me that she owns a small shop in Bissau and travels back and forth, twice a year. Every time she goes, she explained, she is struck by the number of needy children in her home country. She shared with me her dream of working together with Ned and me to create an NGO to help them. She could handle the situation on the ground in Guinea-Bissau, and Ned and I could assist with the planning, advertising, and fundraising. I enthusiastically agreed and look forward to the challenges and rewards of this project. Aside from turning Fatima's dream into a reality, it would also take my own compensatory efforts to the next level: from material and non-material means of "predestined help" to collaborative projects of research participants' own imagining.

NOTES

1. I presented a draft of the conference-paper version of this chapter in ANTH/SOCI 201: Field Research in Local Communities at Bucknell University in Spring 2017. I am grateful for my students' attention and helpful feedback. In particular, comments from Robert Fornshell, Lisa Jouravleva, Jake Kennedy, Anthony Scrima, and Abbie Titus greatly improved the organization and argument. I presented a revised version at the 2017 annual meeting of the Society for Applied Anthropology in Santa Fe. I would like to thank Alma Gottlieb for her engaging discussant remarks and Rory Turner, Josh Fisher, and Ned Searles for their questions and comments, which helped me move the work from conference paper to book chapter. Ned Searles read the first draft and helped me to tighten the language and sharpen the analytical points. Most of all, I am indebted to my research participants in Bissau, Bafata-Oio,

and Lisbon, whose lives over the past two decades have become intertwined with mine in ways that I could have never imagined when I began my fieldwork. I dedicate this article to all of them, but especially to the late Al-Hajj Fodimaye Turé, Numoo Turé, Saajo Daabo, Maternal Kin Club members in Lisbon, and my two namesakes, White Fatumata in Bafata-Oio and Fatumata in Lisbon.

2. In her work in Tanzania, Fourshey (2012) describes hospitality—which "encompasses kindness, generosity, and welcoming towards outsiders"—(2012:23) as a "trademark practice of Africans" (2012:20). Considering this historical perspective, Islam might have intensified a preexisting African ethos of hospitality.

3. Pink (1998:9) challenges the very notion of exchange inherent in anthropological research. She views the idea that anthropologists take something from the community in which they work (i.e., "data") and feel obligated to "give something back" as compensation for this as inherently problematic.

4. See Hutchinson (1996, Ch. 2) for a discussion of the meaning of money, especially the difference between cattle and cash, among Nuer peoples in Sudan.

5. This practice is reminiscent of Mauss's classic work (1950) on gift exchange: "To accept something from somebody is to accept some part of his spiritual essence, of his soul" (1990:12). Mauss explained that in many societies, time was also a crucial element in reciprocating gifts.

6. See Gottlieb (2012a) for reflections on the challenges of compensation when the anthropologist "studies up." In Gottlieb's case, she went from working with Beng villagers in Côte d'Ivoire to working in Lisbon with highly mobile, educated, elite Cape Verdeans.

7. Bertin graduated from the University of Illinois and become the first Beng person to receive a university degree. He later obtained his PhD and is now a professor.

8. Amilcar Cabral University, Guinea-Bissau's first public university, opened in 2003.

9. When Gottlieb and Graham returned to Côte d'Ivoire, their six-year-old son, Nathaniel, received a Beng name. Aba Kouassi, the chief priest of the village of Asagbé where Gottlieb conducted her fieldwork, had a dream in which N'zri Denju, an ancestor, came to him. "Grandfather Denju" told him that he had returned to life as Nathaniel. So, Nathaniel was given the name N'zri Denju, which would shape the way Alma and Philip could treat their son: they would call him "Grandpa" and could never hit him (see Gottlieb and Graham 2012:40–43).

10. Pink (1998:14) argues that "helping" does not have the same universal meanings in other cultures and what the anthropologist "gives back" to research participants is often invested with different meanings and can be used in ways unintended by the anthropologist.

Chapter 3

Existential Debt

How Race and History Complicate the Legibility of the Gift

Carolyn M. Rouse

PAN-AFRICAN GLOBAL ACADEMY

In 2008, I started building a high school on the western edge of Accra, Ghana. I was asked by the chief, elders, and many members of the community to build it. While designing this research project, which doubled as a gift, many anthropologists felt a need to warn me about how misdirected I was. The idea that an anthropologist with power (me) would build a school for those without power (Ghanaians) was a prima facie case of neocolonialism. People asked me, "Haven't you read James Ferguson, Arturo Escobar, and other scholars who have shown that by participating in international development you are complicit in forms of imperialism?"

"Yes," I would tell them. "I have read the anthropological critiques, love the work, and have taught numerous books and articles challenging foreign aid." They would sometimes continue their criticisms by noting that being an American in Ghana, I was, by definition, a destructive force.

Building a high school in Ghana was certainly the most difficult project I have ever undertaken, and I unwittingly became entangled in community destruction and violence because of the land occupied by the school. The land issues I faced were tied to a chieftaincy dispute in Oshiyie that started long before I got there, a dispute that continued well after my involvement with the school diminished to working with the headmaster on schooling data. Despite the early difficulties, the high school is doing well more than a decade later and has graduated more than 150 students in seven classes. Many are now attending college.

I start my chapter with an elliptical narrative of a very complicated story of reciprocity. I do so because the details of what some might call my (mis) adventure include politics, land appropriation, and violence. Elsewhere I have written about how my gift produced unintended consequences, but the land issues and cyclical community violence were only my fault in the sense that I chose to work with a community that had these issues (Rouse, 2014). At the time, my lawyer estimated that 80 percent of court cases in Ghana involved land disputes. That said, I certainly was not free of blame.

Responding to my anthropologist critics, I would typically state that I was aware of my indeterminate subject position(s) while engaging in a "development" project. I certainly had forms of power that my interlocutors did not have. I took their images at moments of vulnerability. My Ghanaian research assistants sometimes logged interview numbers on the walls of their houses in charcoal. I encouraged fisherman and poor petty traders to give up their children's day labor for a future with few guarantees. I questioned their use of time and their choice of exchange practices. Regardless of my race and gender, I was privileged by my citizenship and relative wealth; two of many unavoidable power differentials in the field. In "Processing Privilege: Reflections on Fieldwork (Early, and otherwise) among Beng Villagers of Cote d'Ivoire," Alma Gottlieb (2018) details the near impossibility of downplaying one's privilege in the field. The fact that I even felt entitled to try to "save the world" speaks to power inequities between me and my interlocutors. At the same time, I did all of this while building a high school at their request. I would argue, in fact, that my interlocutors also had forms of power that I did not; an observation articulated by anthropologist Jennifer Nourse (2002) in "Who's Exploiting Whom? Agency, Fieldwork, and Representations among Lauje of Indonesia."

What I struggled to get across to my anthropologist critics is that I agreed with them on many levels. But characterizing contemporary foreign aid, charity, and NGO non-profit work in formerly colonized countries as neocolonial or neo-imperial is too facile. Of course, many projects have been carried out in bad faith, and failure has been the norm (Ferguson, 2006; Escobar, 1995; Karim, 2011; Easterly, 2006; Moyo, 2009; Munk, 2013). That said, sub-Saharan Africa is radically different now than it was sixty years ago, which means that development is happening in ways that the critics and the metrics are unable to capture (Zeleza, 2019). Through the experience of building a school, I wanted to reconcile the divide between the quantitative metrics and the experience of living in an increasingly "developed" West Africa.

Another way of looking at building the school is that rather than (or perhaps in addition to) being a neo-imperialist project, it simply flipped the act of reciprocity. I paid my debt up front knowing that it is impossible to conduct long-term anthropological research without being obliged to give back. The difference in my case was the size of the gift, and the fact that the gift was also my object of study. This doubling of gift/project infuriated one anonymous reader of my book manuscript, who said, "Given all the terrible things done in the world based on this kind of logic, perhaps this is the real hubris alluded to in the book's title." In many ways, this chapter is my attempt to think more deeply about development hubris and reciprocity in light of this criticism.

My sense throughout my fieldwork was that my race and gender made it more difficult for me to relate to the criticism. And it was not just my intersectional identities that made it difficult to relate. I also knew that the power I had over my interlocutors was never unidirectional. In fact, the people I worked with in Oshiyie had a hard time connecting me to my gift. I did not resemble or act like the iconic development worker, so it was difficult to know if the school was a state, business, or aid project. It was also difficult to know what my role was since I would quietly work with the headmaster during my twice-yearly month-long trips. And when the headmaster, David, put up a billboard for the school along the main road, he used a photo of one of my white students—not me, an Ashesi University (black) student, or my Asian American student. David knew that my white student's race would immediately be legible, marking the school as a development aid project linked to Europe or the United States.

Being an African American anthropologist, I was differently positioned by Ghanaians with respect to Western colonialism/development or the project of saving black souls via a mandate to civilize the "other." That did not, however, mean that I was innocent or incapable of condescension, or of promoting neocolonialism. I recognized the problems with gifts of foreign aid in West Africa, which is why, in the next section, I present my own critique of "do gooder" development. If the legibility of the gift requires understanding the intentions of the giver, I need to state my intentions clearly for the record. Like my critics, I too have problems with development practices. Many projects, from large aid regime interventions to small charities, are shot through with racism and ethnocentrism.

What follows is an attempt to unpack the layered, contradictory, and problematic aspects of my motivations to pair a study of development with the gift of a high school. I highlight how my race and gender informed my approach to working with the community, but how those identities also made the gift illegible as such. I begin by presenting a bit more of the background of the project starting with my awakening to the racialized aspects of the late twentieth-century, early twenty-first-century, "do-gooder" ethic; an ethic that, in many respects, I have embraced. I then present a more detailed ethnography of my work in order to highlight the personal and professional stakes. Finally, I end with an analysis of my personal existential motivations that are a product of American racial history, and my sense that one should always use one's power and skills, in some measure, to make the world a better place for the most number of people.[1]

UNPACKING THE RACIALISM IN "DOING GOOD"

If you spent any time in the halls of a university in the first decade of the twenty-first century, you probably saw posters advertising travel abroad to some developing nation, often to help change the lives of poor women and children. These advertisements, with rare exception, had an image of a young, light-skinned student, more than likely female, surrounded by a group of brown-skinned, smiling children. The people in the photo were rarely iden-tified, and race was used as shorthand to communicate who was doing the rescuing and who needed saving. These generic ads provided so little infor-mation that in order to make sense of them, the casual reader had to use his or her imagination to fill in the gaps. The reader's imagination was critical to building a coherent narrative of doing good in the world. Importantly, these programs, derisively called drive-by development or slum tourism, were an industry fueled by the imagination.

A small percentage of these photos included dark-skinned aid workers. These images confused the viewer, forcing him or her to ask, "Who is help-ing whom?" The black aid worker did more than just confuse the viewer. Whether we are willing to admit it or not, skin color was important to the story that the photos were trying to tell. The white student, teacher, or aid worker stood in for Western enlightenment, modernity, rationality, and Judeo-Christian compassion. Without such a powerful narrative behind these otherwise mundane group photos, these programs, initiatives, interventions, engagements—whatever you want to call them—would not make sense.

Fueled by a sense that middle-class Americans had the power to save the world, these programs were not a historical accident. These small-scale international charitable engagements fascinate me because they started when images of third-world suffering began to circulate widely. In the late 1960s and early 1970s, images of starving Biafrans were quickly followed by images of Ethiopian famine victims (Sontag, 2004). Photojournalism was not new, but the sheer volume, the move from black and white to color, and the detailed reporting, brought distant suffering into the homes of middle-class Americans (Boltanski, 1999).

Strangely, the philanthropic ethic ignited by this sense of compassion for strangers was at odds with our national and foreign policy. The suf-fering that ordinary Americans tried to end hardly compared to the suffer-ing the U.S. government caused by destabilizing poor countries, such as Vietnam. Moreover, the many Americans who participated in these charitable adventures seemed tone-deaf to the poverty and racism in their own back-yards. Even decades after this media-inspired charitable ethic emerged, the most vexing aspects of this billion-dollar-a-year industry was the continued lack of reflection about what we were doing, why we were doing it, and if we were helping in the ways we imagined (Donnelly, 2012).

Questions about the rationale and promises of small-scale development have been with me since I was the first brown-skinned student to participate in School for Field Studies (SFS) in Kenya in 1985. For one semester, a group of us, all American college students, stayed at a game ranch outside Nairobi where the owner sustainably husbanded game animals, so we were told. He then sold the meat to tourists in the city.

The SFS program in Kenya was sold as an opportunity for students to study the causes for the expansion of the Sahel. In the 1980s, overgrazing, soil sali-nization, and topsoil erosion were blamed for turning once fertile areas into deserts. Now with a greater focus on the role of greenhouse gas emissions in climate change around the world, the causes for desertification are more hotly debated. But at the time, we were taught that animal domestication and land settlements were to blame. Cattle are part of a group of hooved mammals known as ungulates. Unlike zebra, giraffe, wildebeest, and other ungulates indigenous to East Africa, cattle require up to 10 gallons of water per day to survive. Their thirst means that they are poorly adapted for East Africa. The scientific details were less important than the logic of the SFS narrative. We came to Kenya to reassert the need to get (black) Kenyans to change their culture, for their own good, of course.

As students, we worked in the abattoir, a word with a lyrical quality that misrepresents the horror of bloody floors and dismembered animal parts. One evening a week on the ranch, a group of Kenyans would hunt a herd of indigenous ungulates that could be thinned sustainably: one week, ante-lope; the next week, wildebeest; the next, giraffe. The carcass would then be loaded onto a truck and driven to the abattoir. Once the animal had been dismembered, we would study the parts of the slaughtered animal in order to learn how their bodies were better adapted to drier climates. What we did not appreciate at the time was that what was really being sustained was an exotic meat market for tourists in Nairobi.

As the semester wore on, I became increasingly skeptical. For one, the environmental mission was utterly divorced from the past and present political and social concerns of Kenyans. I was appalled, in particular, by how the black Kenyan employees were treated given the claim that the ultimate purpose of our scientific mission was to empower Kenyans by showing them how to preserve pastoral lands. At a personal level, it did not help that one white American teacher told me that I looked like Aunt Jemima, and that the British-Kenyan owner of the game ranch described the black Kenyans as apes. Comments like these were explicit examples of the implicit claims about racial superiority that, at the time, was sold as sustainable development.

SFS has since cut ties with the game ranch, most certainly has improved its program, and by now has probably welcomed many more black Americans as participants. I say this because, as painful an experience as it was, I look back on it with gratitude for changing my life. It was while walking in a field of tall grass with Peter, a black Kenyan who worked on the ranch, that I had an epiphany that I wanted to study anthropology and film. I stayed behind on the ranch and talked to Peter whenever the other students went shopping in Nairobi. I took time out to visit his church where I had my first experience with Pentecostalism. Peter and I needed to affirm that black Africans and black Americans had each other's back, so to speak.

At the time, I personalized the racial issues I experienced in the program as an attack on me. It was only after returning to college and taking a class on African literature and history with exiled South African writer Dennis Brutus that I came to appreciate the racialized foundations of most development work in sub-Saharan Africa. Many of the charitable interventions sold by money-making educational or community service programs continue to rely on narratives that collapse intellectual and moral capacity with race and gender. Consider again the photos for charitable field experiences adorning college halls. How do you know that the white student has knowledge that the brown or black child/adult wants or needs? Do girls and women—brown, black, and Muslim—need to be rescued (see Abu-Lughod, 2013)? Do boys and men—brown, black, and Muslim—need help, as well? What is it that we are trying to do, given that significant social change is generally the result of state projects such as roads, airports, and dams?

Years later, my decision to go to Ghana to participate in the building of a school was motivated, in part, by my effort to redo my earlier experience in Kenya. My sense was that the desire to make the world a better place was still valid. What I needed this time was to reject the ethnocentrism, racism, and progress narratives embedded in development discourses (Pierre, 2019; Rist, 2002). My thought was that my experience would give me the evidence I needed to argue that development discourses are not only self-serving misreadings of cultural history by Westerners, but that the explicit and implicit assertations in the discourses reproduce black racial inequalities globally (Ashraf and Galor, 2013; Levi-Strauss, 1952; Rouse, 2019).

THE SCHOLARLY AND PERSONAL STAKES

I founded Pan African Global Academy (PAGA) because at a town meeting in 2006 many of the women and elders of the community asked me to build it. At the time, the Ghanaian government only funded around 400 public high schools throughout the country and most were underfunded and of varying quality. At the same time, schooling was in high demand because it was seen as the best guarantee of future job security. In *Dilemmas of Culture in African Schools: Youth, Nationalism, and the Transformation of Knowledge*, anthropologist Cati Coe describes how schooling is also considered a site for producing a national culture and imparting religious/spiritual values, often seen as one and the same (Coe, 2005). Moreover, parents who make sure that their children are educated are viewed as modern or developed, which is another reason that so many Ghanaian parents are willing to spend a large percentage of their income on secondary education.

PAGA, which officially started in 2010, was meant to reduce barriers to schooling by reducing tuition and eliminating transportation fees. Parents willingly paid for long commutes to high schools closer to downtown Accra. PAGA is in a fishing village about 20 kilometers from the center of Accra. In 2010, the students paid a tuition fee of 100 Ghana Cedis per year, about $90 at the time. Equivalent schools were charging around $400 per year in tuition. The rate of about $90 remains. The fees were necessary because the school was not built on a charity model, and local tax revenue was not allocated to help subsidize high school education. I knew this because the Oshiyie's tax collector, the chief's cousin, told me that most of the revenue went to the state and what remained went mainly to fund festivities related to Homowo, a set of rituals celebrating Ga migration and survival that runs from May through September.

Building the school required not only meeting the students' educational needs through curricular design, it also meant building the school on land designated by the community's urban blueprint. On their suggestion, I agreed to build the school next to the junior high school, but the elders insisted that the high school students wanted their own campus, away from the younger children. My lawyer for the project discovered that it was the same land purchased years ago by a Ghanaian returnee, back from England. He purchased it from the chief after promising to build a high school for the community. In fact, this returnee nicknamed "Burger," a term commonly used for returnees, had purchased over fifty plots of land. He promised he would build estate houses, and every tenth house would be given to an elder for free. Burger did none of this. Instead, he titled the land officially through the Lands Commission and then sold it to wealthy outsiders to enrich himself. The chief signed the land over to me to take it away from Burger, who had not fulfilled his promise.

Since the land had been formally titled in Burger's name, I had to buy the land back from him. Then in 2009, when I was ready to begin building, heads of a few of the clans demanded that I pay them, arguing that the land was "family land" and not "stool land," meaning that the chief did not have the authority to sell the land or designate it for a school. In the end, I purchased the land twice in order to build PAGA.

GIFT/PROJECT: STRUGGLES WITH
TRANSLATION AND LEGIBILITY

The story of how PAGA came to be is so complicated and nuanced that it is impossible for me to tell just a portion without confusing (or angering) readers. Elsewhere, I detail the history of the project, but in this chapter, I abbreviate the story by jumping to the end to let the reader know that things worked out. I do so in order to foreground other parts of my adventure that often get lost in the details. Here, I offer a meditation on the legibility of gifting and reciprocity in the field. I consider whether or not the gifts that anthropologists offer are understood in the ways we think they are, as gifts. Lost, in particular, is the question of whether the school was a gift, a reparation, or a political project. I had my own ideas, but it became clear that translating my motivations was much more difficult than I had imagined. Ghanaians did not read the school as a gift because many did not see me, an African American woman, as being powerful or capable enough to complete such a project. Most thought that I was an employee of some powerful American entity for which I was simply doing my job. Since I was a professor at Princeton University and had funded the construction of the school with grant money, in some respect they were right. But the relationship was indirect.

Many anthropologists also did not see the school as a gift. To them, it was a neocolonial project that would aid in the further disempowerment of the community—in other words, a Trojan Horse. My race and gender were considered inconsequential relative to my American citizenship, which linked me to American imperialism. I was repeatedly told, explicitly, that my project was a neocolonial one.

Whatever I thought I was doing, gifting or reciprocating, was unreadable as such. This has to do largely with cultural expectations around gifting. In most societies, rules surrounding gifting generally do not require less powerful individuals, a niece, for example, to reciprocate the gift of a more powerful senior, such as an uncle (Bateson, 1936). Like joking relationships, gifting has a form that makes the exchange—in one case, reciprocity and in the other, bawdy humor—culturally acceptable and intelligible (Thomson, 1935). In my case, the situation was confusing because it was not clear to my interlocutors that I was more powerful than they, so why was I gifting them this gift? In addition to my race and gender, I took shared vans (*trotros*) for transportation rather than driving an SUV, the car model of choice for most development workers in Africa. Also, the ability to mobilize people is associated with power, but I worked alone without an entourage. Finally, I helped dig in the school garden, an activity that a woman with stature delegates.

Based on the context and the individuals involved, a gift can be (mis)read as an obligation, a reparation, a remediation, or even an act of condescension, particularly in cross-cultural settings with complicated histories and power dynamics. In postcolonial Ghana, where there is a heavy presence of foreign aid workers and NGO development projects, it is difficult to distinguish everyday forms of gifting from charity, foreign aid, entitlements, or reparations. This confusion stems in part from, as Jemima Pierre (2019) describes, the vernaculars of development, which use the condescending language of aid to mask resource theft and human exploitation. During colonialism, the gift of religious salvation and civilization justified the same things. My critics sensed a similar masking in my project, but I would argue that the critique makes blanket assumptions about identity and power, assumptions that were not observable in the field.

In order to move past the critique of my project as a neocolonial one, I highlight a bit more about where the project is in its second decade. At this point, the school is in no way mine. Since it started in 2010, it has been run by my brilliant friend, Headmaster David Lamptey, a chemist trained at Kwame Nkrumah University of Science and Technology. I still help fund projects run by Princeton University and Ashesi University students. For example, students have built a wind turbine on the campus, which helped the school through many blackouts. Ashesi and Princeton University students also designed the school's project-based, Science Technology Engineering Arts and Math (STEAM-based) curriculum. These college students have taught computer science, math, accounting, and social studies, but, more importantly, they have learned. The biggest lesson they have taken away from the community and the project is that theories of development do not map cleanly onto experience. Social histories and people are complicated.

At this point, the Parent Teachers Association (PTA) and the Headmaster make key decisions. And if a Princeton University student suggests a project that David and I think would be good for the school, we help the student get internship funding. In 2015, some of the residents suggested naming the road running from the downtown straight up to the school PAGA Road, after the school. Others wanted to name it after the televangelist who had recently finished building three huge estate houses next to the school (after the school was completed, estate houses began popping up around the school). Importantly, the community I walked into in 2006 has radically changed, as has the Ghanaian government's commitment to funding high school. With all of these changes have come changes to the meaning and value of the original gift. Nobody in the community feels they owe me a debt, which is exactly how I wanted it.

What I hope readers note is that power was, in my case, complicated. As Michel Foucault might say, it circulated. My sense was that if the community really did not want the school for their children, they would have stopped it by refusing to participate (Collins, 1998; Scott, 1985). The parents knew in general what they wanted for their children and I provided some of the specifics. While the school was not my choice alone, education as a project makes sense to me for personal reasons. My great-grandfather was shot and killed in Cherokee, Alabama in part for his efforts to obtain schooling for his children. Trying to teach got Antonio Gramsci and Paulo Freire thrown into prison. As Freire said when discussing the role education could play in freeing people from abjection, "Freedom is acquired by conquest, not by gift" (Freire 2000:47).

One cannot participate/engage/collaborate in an educational project without having to struggle with power, one's own and others. Certainly, power exists and has real effects, but power is indeterminant, which means that knowing that power matters should not determine what anthropologists should and should not do. When it comes to development, whether in our backyard or someone else's, the quality of our engagements should be the focus of our critique not only the end results.

The fact that I could fly away from my fieldsite really bothered some of my critics. It seemed to be the ultimate sign of my privilege, which, shame on me, I failed to grasp. But I never saw my interlocutors as powerless. In fact, in many instances, they had power over me. Importantly, I was doing their bidding by building a school that they asked me to build on a plot of land that they had designated. And the community violence, where clan members only attacked one another and not new arrivals to the community, was a constant reminder that sometimes outsiders are seen as less threatening than are neighbors and extended kin.

My purpose in writing this chapter is to challenge anthropological critiques who presume that development aid is read as a gift by those who receive it—a gift that indebts nations and individuals who are incapable of repayment. This unpaid debt obligation, real and existential, further cements unequal power dynamics between countries, between foreign aid donors and recipients, and between individuals differently situated within this binary. Rather than living in a persistent sense of indebtedness, individuals in Oshiyie freely interpreted the school "gift" any way they wanted to. The fact that I was African American made it easier to reinterpret the gift. For those who saw the school as a reparation, rather than a gift, my project had no power over them and the "spirit of the gift," as Mauss (2016[1925]) would have termed it, never materialized. In household surveys that I conducted in 2008 before the land issues were even settled, parents wondered why it was taking so long to build the school. In complaints about the project, people described education as a right, not a gift, and they therefore saw the school as the fulfillment of a prior obligation by the Ghanaian state and/or former colonial powers.

The legibility of my school project, in other words, was complicated by the power relationships linked to social identities and histories that cross the Atlantic. Whereas I saw the school as a way to reciprocate the community's gift of engagement, the community saw the school as their right. I argue that this was in part due to the fact that my identity did not easily map onto standard cultural narratives about development aid and gifting. In my case, local interpretations of the school as something other than a gift were in part linked to a refusal to be dominated, and in part linked to a missing cultural narrative about African Americans' obligation to "give back" to Africa. This reading made my gifting illegible as such. At one point I privately told the Oshiyie lawyer, who for decades had helped the chiefs manage the community lands, that in my four years working on the project nobody had thanked me. He felt bad for me and so took me out to dinner. It was perhaps the most awkward dinner I have ever had given that he owed me nothing and we both knew that. By begging for reciprocity, I took on another debt. As we sat alone, the only diners in the restaurant, it occurred to me that even though I entered the field thinking that the school was a gift, perhaps part of the illegibility had to do with the fact that I did not want people to see it as a gift. In some respects, I felt the project was part of my existential obligation to give back to the world in whatever way I could.

EXISTENTIAL DEBTS AND GLOBAL BLACKNESS

Regardless of how I felt about what I was doing, many anthropologists accused me of having the same motivations and lack of reflexivity as the development apparatus that gave us structural adjustments. My racial position in the United States and all the attendant histories and daily struggles did not matter to my critics. Being told, essentially, that an identity so central to who I considered myself to be was irrelevant was profoundly disorienting but useful to think with.

Over the years, my experiences around race in Ghana have been complex. No Ghanaians, for example, screamed at me about my role in under-developing Africa, which happened on occasion to the white students I brought to Ghana. My race and gender meant that I did not stand in for colonial history and was positioned differently with respect to American power. In *The Predicament of Blackness in Post-colonial Ghana*, Jemima Pierre (2013) describes how black and white Americans are treated and interpreted differently in Ghana. Pierre's analysis is an important contribution to new studies of what is called global blackness: how skin color rather than cultural traits situates people differently around the world. Many African Studies scholars disagree with Pierre's analysis and argue for a more Marxian class analysis of hierarchy in Africa. Given my experiences, I would argue that both skin color and class matter in many postcolonial countries. Importantly, even though Ghanaians considered my existential and material debts lower than that of whites because of my race, Ghanaians did not see me as their equal. They often treated me like a long-lost friend, or perhaps a wealthy cousin from the United States, but I was rarely afforded the deference reserved for white Westerners, who were considered uniquely powerful unless they were dressed like "hippies" and carried backpacks (Pierre, 2013).

I was radically "other," which meant that my existential debts were difficult to enumerate. There are no historical ledgers that calculate what African Americans owe Africans, and without a clear accounting, our commitments and obligations must be improvised. I knew for research purposes that I needed to reflexively articulate the origins of my sense of obligation. Ultimately, I traced my existential motivations to African American history and the obligation African American intellectuals have felt since the nineteenth century to use their scholarship for positive social change. "Giving back" within the United States makes some sense—but, why Ghana?

The history of slavery, colonialism, and development has complicated the story of whiteness and blackness around the world (Bashkow, 2017; Gilroy 1991, 1993; Pierre, 2013). In the United States, I am identified as African American. In Ghana I am an Obroni, a term meaning "foreign" and "white" interchangeably, but not specifically African American. "There goes that Obroni who is building the school," people would say. What does this identification mean? Sadly, I discovered that, for the most part, it is better to be identified with white Americans and Europeans than with African Americans. In Ghana, I experienced what Randy Matory describes as *ethnological schadenfreude*, an ethno-racial distancing used to differentiate marginalized groups. The anxieties produced by racism occasion racial refashioning by black Americans and black Africans alike (Matory, 2015). Many Ghanaians wanted to make clear that my skin color did *not* align us, like the drummer Ghanaba who described black Americans as "racists, fucking racists" to white anthropologist Steven Feld (Feld 2012:53). Ghanaba repeatedly noted to Feld how much he despised "AMERICAN Jazz bullshit." (Feld 2012:55). Black Americans take pride in the fact that they are not from "the jungle" and lay claim to cultural and educational superiority.

Globally, African Americans are the *iconic other* whom people around the world love to borrow but would prefer not to be (Holsey, 2013). Who wants to be associated with a disproportionately disfranchised lot such as the

Roma, the Dalit, or the Ainu? I learned this in 2008 at the start of my project. I also learned, however, that black/white issues are far more complicated than simply the valorization of whiteness. In Ghana, whiteness is also associated with colonization.

While I was describing the history of Motown, a Ghanaian man I had been working with for a month interrupted me with an urgent question, "You're black?" On the street, people called me Obroni, but I translated that as foreigner. I did not think that anyone actually considered me white given my complexion. I looked at both of my arms and said, "Yeah." He said, "I thought you just got tan from the sun." The conversation died, replaced by stunned silence rather than laughter, which, I thought, would have been more appropriate. Being separated from my history was disarming. It became clear that I was marked as both colonizer and colonized, a double negative, matter and antimatter, a hapless non-entity who was coming to recolonize Ghana.

In order to gift in a way that is legible, and that makes the receiver feel obligated to reciprocate (or not), one needs to occupy a legible social space (Malinowski 1984[1922]; Bateson, 1936; Mauss 2016[1925]). But who was I? As I already noted, African Americans are not indebted to Africans historically. And in terms of the aid regime, most Ghanaians associate development with white Europeans and Americans. I also made myself illegible by never attending celebrations of our school accomplishments; I left that for David to do. The first celebration I attended was the first graduation in 2014. By then, the school was understood as a project funded by the elders. I encouraged this narrative for reasons too numerous to describe, but primarily having to do with my desire for the community to have a sense of ownership over the project. I did not try to make myself more legible to the community because my entire project was meant to find a way to disrupt the power dynamics in "doing good." Despite my intentions, my anthropologist critics dispute that I could be anything other than an American imperialist.

SETTLING MY PROFESSIONAL DEBTS

My rationale for participating in an international development project was based on my critique of three contemporary discourses within anthropology, a discipline to which I feel indebted. First, I rejected the notion that development can be understood as either success or failure. Development is a process of continual adaptation to new norms. Even what we consider to be a successful development project, one that has withstood the test of time, is never what it was at the beginning. Any successful development project must always deal with successive "failures," or projects, activities, and resource allocations that no longer make sense. Successful organizations constantly recalibrate their mission to attend to the fact that people come and go and adjacent institutions as well as economic and social needs change. Even environmental change can create new constraints and possibilities. In sum, the idea that a development project "failed" is historically interesting but often theoretically beside the point.

The second powerful anthropological discourse I pushed back against was the idea that participating in international development was akin to being a neo-imperialist. In the 1990s, anthropologists James Ferguson (1994) and Arturo Escobar (1995) brilliantly critiqued discourses of underdevelopment, modernization theory, and attempts to bypass politics through neoliberal approaches to economic development. As a result of the power of Ferguson's and Escobar's scholarship, some scholars began to treat their claims, largely historical, as proof that anthropologists should refuse participation in international development on ethical grounds. I know this because anthropologists who participated in such folly, like me, were considered apostates to the discipline and were told so both anonymously and directly.[2]

While I consider the critiques of international aid critically important, any resultant paralysis, or self-satisfied determination to do nothing, did not sit well with me. In terms of human history, development is an ongoing process, given that the material conditions of life are constantly changing. This means that if we choose to do nothing, others are doing something on our behalf. I say this knowing that the fanciful, hubristic, and self-aggrandizing discourses used by NGOs and the aid regime are easy to criticize, like shooting fish in a barrel. But as much as we like to make fun of these discourses ("One laptop per child . . ." really?), deciding how to approach the future requires an active imagination animated by value propositions, creative uses of data, and great leaps of faith. How else can one confront the unknown or, more importantly, rally people to collectively confront the unknown? As development expert Gilbert Rist notes, development is a "faith." In his book, *The History of Development*, Rist (2002) characterizes faith as a weakness, whereas I consider faith essential to human organization and survival. Faith, in other words, is not a bug, but a feature of development.

Given my sense that development must be understood as a human problem, I do not consider applied anthropologists guiltier of neo-imperialism than, say, economists, sociologists, political scientists, or psychologists. At times, members of our discipline have wandered into ugly political projects including colonialism, eugenics, spying, and now the Human Terrain System, but the American Anthropological Association (AAA) is perhaps the one social science association that has made efforts to learn from its past. Economics and political science, on the other hand, have done far more with respect to shaping neo-imperialist policies and practices around the world than has anthropology. Anthropologists have not always been innocent observers but most applied anthropologists are attentive to and concerned about the oppressive forces impacting the lives of their interlocutors/stakeholders.

Finally, my research pushed back against a presumption about who should and should not participate in local development projects. The idea that strangers or foreigners should not do so for ethical reasons disrupts everything we know about human migration, cultural diffusion, and the role that formal and informal law have played in integrating strangers throughout history.[3] Strangers were often welcomed because they brought new ideas and materials. Rather than disrupting the group, strangers often reinforce the identity of the groups they encounter even as they precipitate cultural change. We see this in the case of immigrants to the United States. And eventually, strangers become friends, fictive kin, or sometimes even kin (Gottlieb 2004).

In addition to objecting to the arguments that international development 1) is unethical; 2) is by definition imperialism; and 3) is always a negative force in local politics, I objected to the idea that all Americans are similarly situated with respect to American exceptionalism and imperialism. I am an African American and that matters. I, too, have been subjected to American projects to civilize unruly brown and black people. The discourses of Western/white supremacy have only worked against me, so I was certainly not motivated by modernization theory.

For me, the existential questions of reparations were far less important than the pragmatic issues of the usefulness of education for those who might otherwise be crushed by powerful international markets. Importantly, many members of the community were selling their land when they thought they were just leasing it. So, something as simple as knowing how to read, knowing something about changes in property law, and knowing how to estimate the value of land in the present and future seemed to be important for pragmatic reasons. I was not the one to teach Ghanaian high school students, but I could be the outsider who helps a community organize and structure resources so that they can.

CONCLUSION: REPARATIONS AS AN EVERYDAY HUMANISTIC PROJECT

Being African American, I do not associate being in America with the same sense of privilege and entitlement that perhaps some of my white colleagues do. I am constantly reminded that I do not fully belong. Reminders come in the form of mass incarceration, numerous scholarly books claiming low IQ among blacks, cultural dysfunction, and even the policing in stores that require me to perform particular tricks so that store clerks do not feel threatened. Given my experiences with race in the United States, I feel no sense of responsibility for past colonialism or imperialism in the same way that I do not feel anger toward West Africans whose ancestors sold my ancestors to slave traders. Importantly, my decision to gift a school in Ghana was in no way an act of personal or political redemption. In fact, at times the school felt like an obligation. I had grown up believing that any paid employment had to, in part, be directed toward making the world a better place. My scholarship on racial inequality, therefore, had to be put toward applying what I knew toward ameliorating disparities, in this case, educational and economic ones.

For me, the point of building a school in Ghana was to theorize development from the perspective of the embodied act of doing. Given this experience, when I teach about development I now start by highlighting that development is an inevitable human process that involves, at once, gifting, power, and imagination. Beyond questions of development failure or success lie existential questions about the greater purpose of knowledge production and our relationships to others, including strangers. In other words, development, like gifting, is a human problem with spatial, temporal, affective, and political dimensions that speak to assemblages that also include race, gender, and historical subjectivities.

In Achille Mbembe's (2017) *The Critique of Black Reason*, a text in which he critiques race as a fiction, he writes about how racism has been useful for state projects that treat certain bodies as expendable, or necropolitics. He also addresses the question of how we repair the damage caused by political projects mobilized by these fictions. While he argues for a kind of reparative justice, Mbembe says we must break free of the notion that we owe justice only to those of our own race. He writes (2017:178):

> On the one hand, we must escape the status of victimhood. On the other, we must make a break with "good conscious" and the denial of responsibility. It is through this dual approach that we will be able to articulate a new politics and ethics founded on a call for justice . . . . What we must imagine is a politics of humanity that is fundamentally a politics of the similar, but in a context in which what we all share from the beginning is difference. It is our differences that, paradoxically, we must share. And all of this depends on reparations, on the expansion of our conception of justice and responsibility.

My school was, importantly, not an act of "reparation" in the sense of a repayment for a debt; it was supposed to be a project motivated by my concerns with justice and responsibility, as articulated by Mbembe. Existentially, I have no sense that I owe Ghanaians for what Europe and the United States have done to poorer countries in the name of development. Rather, I feel debt as human. What I know about social justice is that asymmetries in knowledge and power allow for the continued exploitation of certain people, including theft of their land. Having grown up in a wealthy country that protects its wealth through necropolitics, it is my responsibility to sacrifice what I can, as best I can, to push back against exploitation. And, selfishly, I do that because if development discourses such as modernization theory can dehumanize blacks in other countries, then I know that those same discourses can be used to dehumanize me. That is how black reason has worked as a rationale for the exploitation of certain bodies based on their supposed inferiority.

So, I feel my debt is partly repaid every time I hear that another student from my school in Ghana has matriculated into college, started a business right out of high school, or, as one of my first students did, started teaching at a junior high school just after graduating. My choice to enter the field with a gift originated from assemblages linked to my identity as an African American scholar. My sense of responsibility originated from my belief that as humans, we must do what we can, in whatever capacity afforded us, to expand and sustain the fields of social justice both near and far.

NOTES

1. I would like to thank Michelle Johnson and Ned Searles for their tireless work on getting this collection of chapters to press and my colleagues in Ghana to whom I remain indebted.

2. Interestingly, anthropologists who worked in global health (e.g., Paul Farmer and Jim Kim) were not similarly critiqued. Moreover, many who claimed that foreign aid projects are simply neo-imperialism forgot that around 20 percent of the American Anthropological Association (AAA) members are applied anthropologists. The percentage is even larger if we include anthropologists with postgraduate degrees who are not AAA members. This misrepresentation of American anthropology as a theoretical rather than an applied discipline speaks to larger problems with the critique of forms of community engagement, like my project. Applied anthropology is not beyond criticism, but theory, application, and ethics are not mutually exclusive.

3. By law, I refer to different sources of law, including customary, common, administrative, state, and constitutional law.

Chapter 4

Reflections on a Community of the Heart

The Ethnographer and the People of Juchitán, Oaxaca

Anya Peterson Royce

COMBINED EXPERIENCES, GROWING UNDERSTANDINGS

Being in the field over decades brings challenges and a growing maturity: changes of status for our hosts and for us as ethnographers, a growing ability to see patterns and recognize new questions, experiencing change with them in real time, a more active role in speaking out, and finally, of being given the courage to find your own voice through their example. This is one story of combined experiences and growing understandings.[1]

Juchitán's unique ability to support generations of risk-takers and border-crossers lies in its long history of choosing transformation over stasis. That they have been so successful is a testament to their ability to work as a community while respecting the contribution of each individual member. Seeing this and being part of it over the years has been a remarkable journey.

THE ETHNOGRAPHER AND THE ISTHMUS ZAPOTEC: FIRST ENCOUNTERS

I saw the people of Juchitán for the first time at the 1967 Guelaguetza, an annual festival of the indigenous music and dance of Oaxaca. The Juchitán delegation entered, the women dressed in their most elegant embroidered *trajes* with

Figure 4.1   Delia Ramírez Fuentes, Dancing at the Guelagueta, 1967.

starched white headdresses, the men with their old-style sombreros decorated with heavy silver braids. The dancers were splendid, full of grace and authority. In all that they did, they displayed that kind of assurance that comes with knowing who one is. Their carriage and character were formal yet gracious. The event reflected the importance and gravity of work, or *dxiña*, in maintaining community. That experience erased any idea that I might do research anywhere else. From that moment, my life was inextricably linked with the people of Juchitán, beginning with my Zapotec family, especially Delia Ramírez Fuentes who has become my sister and best friend (see Figure 4.1).

    When I first encountered the people of Juchitán that summer, I was an undergraduate at Stanford University doing my first field research just as I was entering my senior year. To say that I was naïve would be a grave understatement. To assume that I knew then that this would become a lifelong commitment would require prescience that none of us enjoys. It may well be the case, however, that this initial naiveté is what allows us to respond as individuals to other individuals, not as intellects to concepts. In that first encounter, everything is interesting because we have not yet closed our hearts and shuttered our minds with the armor of theoretical paradigms. It was that thrilling moment of having nothing to lose and everything to gain.

The following summer, 1968, my husband, Ronald R. Royce, a linguistic anthropologist, and I came to Juchitán. This was our introduction to the *velas*—the Vela Agosto and the Vela San Jacinto, grand four-day celebrations of a saint, a place, an occupation, or an extended family. *Velas* were then and remain an important focus for me because they support and shape community and the web of connections between individuals and groups. One sees much in the *velas* that defines Juchitán, not only in those tangible manifestations of material culture such as oxcarts, the traditional dress of *huipil* and skirt, fishermen with their nets, the music of the flute and drum, and fireworks of the *regadas*, but also in the traditional music, and in rituals such as the exchange of the *mayordomía* in the all-night dance, dancing (both traditional and popular) in the daytime fiesta, and the custom of offering candles and flowers. Finally, one sees the values of community and of sharing that the *velas* evoke. In those early encounters, only the visible markers were accessible; the meaning behind them took much longer to understand. One of the demands on ethnographers, however, is to record everything, even when you have no sense of what it means or where it fits.

When my mentor, Elizabeth Colson, one of the great ethnographers of a century in which ethnographic field research was what anthropology did, responded to a query from me, she addressed that very sense of being totally at sea. She wrote:

> You say you don't know what to put down because what you hear one day is contradicted by what you hear the next. The only good rule is to put it down—you then put down the next thing you hear. In the end you sort it out and you know which things you misunderstood, where you were deliberately misled (which is interesting), and where the variations come because of the sources of information. Don't wait to write until you are sure you know! And you are quite right. One thing one learns as a field worker is that one is usually wrong and hopefully this is funny. I suppose one learns to overplay the clown as a result. (December 22, 1971)

This was exactly the advice that a new ethnographer needed to hear—Colson said clearly what you must do—write everything down, while not expecting to understand how it all fits (see Royce 2017:142–3). Those notes provide the basis for the analysis that will eventually lead to answering fundamental questions.

WHAT IS THIS SPACE AND SET OF EXPECTATIONS
THAT WE LABEL THE "FIELD"?

Fieldwork has always been what we do—and what we have learned to do—best.
Our theories acquire their strength, elegance, and conviction in accordance with
the quality, honesty, and reliability of our fieldwork. (Mintz 2000:177)

Working in this kind of space is a risky business because, in the thick of
nature and culture, we are not in control. It is precisely this natural environment that lets us hear the material we want to understand in its own setting.
We take it on its own terms, not ours, and see it in all its complexity. We
are forced to confront our own vulnerability and our own humanity in this
interaction. It was not just the Nobel Prize-winning corn geneticist Barbara
McClintock who let corn come to her; it was Barbara McClintock, the person, with all her history, experience, personality, quirks, strengths and weaknesses, who understood her material. Likewise, ethnographers sooner or later
come to understand that it is their whole person who listens to the stories of
other cultures. We are learning substance, but we are also engaged in the
hermeneutics of learning. We reflect on how we know and how who we are
affects what we are coming to understand. As Clifford Geertz (2000:39) commented, ethnographers have to attend to the ordinary business of living at the
same time that they are trying to understand the culture into which they have
inserted themselves. There is something sobering, even bewildering, about
that mundane aspect of our research. I have a point of view that arises out of
my work, but it is work that demands that I be implicated in the life of the
community—body, mind, and heart. This communal participation grows with
the years along with my understanding of details and context.

My husband and I returned to Juchitán for a year in 1971–1972. I was
examining the persistence of Zapotec identity and my husband was focused
on the Zapotec language. My question then and even now was how and
why have the Zapotec people, especially those of Juchitán, been able to
maintain and develop a Zapotec identity while moving freely between this
and a Mexican and global identity when other peoples have not been able to
achieve this. Before coming to Juchitán, Ron and I read everything we could
about the Isthmus and its cultures, including as much archaeology and history
as we could find, and began wrestling with the Isthmus Zapotec language.
But arriving in Juchitán to stay for a year, I felt nervous. The problem for
us as anthropologists is that, in the beginning, we drown in details for which
we have little context. That year, filled with all the homely details of living,
also saw many momentous events: the founding of the Casa de la Cultura,
one of the first in Mexico, and a municipal election in which the Popular
Socialist Party (PPS) appeared in force for the first time. The campaign had

a charismatic leader in the person of Manuel Musalem Santiago, popularly known as "Tarú." He and that election drew national attention to Juchitán once again. It was a baptism of politics and culture. And I now know that these two events remain important touchstones for the Juchitecos.

INTO THE DEEP END: HOW ETHNOGRAPHERS LEARN IN THE FIELD

Children learn to be members of communities by growing up in them learning about everything all the time. By contrast, when we come to a community as fieldworkers, we are plunged in medias res. In that first encounter, we cannot draw boundaries around those things that will be "significant" because we do not know enough to recognize them. We cast a wider net, hoping to be able to build a context into which we can situate our particular interest. We have to be, as Geertz (2000) said, simultaneously engaged and analytic. We are human beings making a life in a community at the same time that we are trying to figure it out. This is a stance that forces us to blunder about searching for anything that might bring order because we are not comfortable with the apparent confusion of a culture whose values we do not yet understand. When I wrote the introductory chapter for *Chronicling Cultures*, an edited volume on long-term field research, I described the neophyte fieldworker's discomfort "with the dynamism and unpredictability of the ethnographic situation, with its swings between the drowse of the accustomed and the chaos of the unexpected" (Royce 2002:xv) and our feeling it necessary to restrain and contain it. I realize now that, in fact, it takes nearly the first year to see even the pattern of the accustomed. Much of what we busy ourselves doing is creating a context in which we can count on certain regularities. We run through the repertory of techniques—mapping spaces, eliciting genealogies, burrowing through archives and records, taking photographs, learning the language, administering surveys, collecting life histories. In the process, we accumulate important data, all the while trying to limit those casual conversations or the small intimacies that are the stuff of human relationship. All these activities in our repertory of methods have one thing in common—they let us imagine ourselves as being in control, or as much in control as we ever are in the field. We exert the same control in our lives out of the community spotlight—prescribed times for writing fieldnotes, the way we arrange our space, hoarding of comfort foods, a sort of talismanic collection of things from home. In the end, however, the ethnographer and the community must engage each other in dialogue, and once you admit the possibility of dialogue, you open the door to the unknown and the unpredictable, inviting what appears to be disorder. While it may seem a stretch to think that we can find commonality with the world of dance, choreography, and how we find a through-line in it, Jonathan Wolken, one of the founders of the Pilobolus Dance Theater, articulated a principle of economy and clarity that applies to field-work. Wolken says:

> In the crush of ideas and individual ideas in our work lives and certainly in our creative lives, we are challenged to hear our own voice over the din of others. For most of our early formative school years we set in motion a process of competitive achievement that sticks with us and colors our habits. We rush forward with answers, we create a blizzard of ideas, we avoid the understated approach by covering it with mass quantities of . . . just about everything. (Interview, August 8, 2008)

For neophyte ethnographers, the problem is that, in the beginning, we drown in details for which we have little context. Often, as Wolken says, we rush forward with answers because we are afraid to admit to ignorance. Wolken continues:

> There is an alternative—a spare and simple approach that appeals to the mind and attracts the eye. We can see this at work on the stage, especially during an improvisation. A glut of activity often serves to hide the best material. The eye simply does not know where to look in the visual cacophony. So, simplify. Unclog, clear away and remove the obstacles that distract from the clarity you seek. (Interview, August 8, 2008)

Wolken is urging less not more and choosing those details that support a through-line, that meaning that lies above the details of the text—in the case of dance, not the individual steps but the meaning of them, or in poetry not the individual words but the larger meaning of them. The result then will be inevitable rather than predictable.

FINDING THE THROUGH-LINE AND MY OWN VOICE

One warm evening, I sat with the governing body of the Vela Igu as they debated the problem of having no sponsor (*mayordomo*) for the coming year. Ta Daniel, eighty-six and the keeper of the *vela*'s histories, listened and then spoke, was sitting close to the ground on the old-style wooden chair and spoke quietly, but commanded everyone's silent attention. He spoke in the old Zapotec, absent Spanish loan words but filled with beautiful images. Ta Daniel's speech was stripped of all non-essentials, elemental, exposing the heart. In the intimacy he held out to every one of us, we realized the simplicity of what was needed. Not a programmatic statement of what to do and how to do it but rather an upwelling of love and faith in this community of the heart. We cover up so much—exaggerate, elaborate, add to—perhaps because we have lost the memory of the heart.

Several weeks passed and I went to sit again with Ta Daniel in the patio of his house, underneath the Jasmine trees, where he told me the history of the Vela Igu and its pilgrimage (see Figure 4.2). His eloquence in describing what the vela meant to him moved me to want to experience this for myself. With my Zapotec sister, Delia, and in honor of Na Rosinda, our mother, I walked the pilgrimage. We left the house of the sponsors just past 6:00 a.m., leaving the city behind as we went into the rural countryside (*gui'xhi* or "wild"). With stops along the way for food and rest and prayer, we arrived at the Chapel of the Crosses at just after 4 in the afternoon. It was in the doing of that, that I realized what all *binniza* know—in order to truly understand, you must plant your feet in the earth of the path, listen to the songs of the prayer-leader, feel the heat, smell the wild, eat the *tamales* offered by pilgrims along the way, arrive at the foot of the mountain, and experience the joy when the big cross meets its brother crosses. That experience changed me profoundly, and stays in my body, heart, and mind.

Figure 4.2   Ta Daniel, Leading the Pilgrimage for the Vela Santa Cruz Igu, 2011.

Experiences crossing between the settled places (*guidxhi*) and the wild (*gui'xhi*) transform us; we need them just as we need food and water. Those who walk the pilgrimages are transformed. Juchitán is blessed, too, with the examples of poets, painters, and musicians who have the courage and curiosity to leap from the known into the unknown. They teach us and give us the courage to place our feet on the path of the stars, trusting in a future that we do not know but that springs from a marvelous antiquity. Their presence is as necessary as the air we breathe.

Acoma Pueblo poet Simon Ortiz captured this essential truth in his poem, "Culture and the Universe," from his collection, *Out There Somewhere* (2002). In the last stanza, he reminds us that it is not culture or society that holds us back, rather it is

It is the vastness we do not enter.
It is the stars we do not let own us.

TELLING THE STORY AND THE
ETHICS OF INTERPRETATION

Writing is hard; in fact, it does not get easier because you must tailor your writing to the story you are telling. As ethnographers, we receive that story as a kind of gift and we have to honor it—so, of course, we are nervous, terrified even, but if we do not tell it, who will? In the end, it is the stories that matter. The metrics play an important role—all those observations, descriptions, archival data, maps, drawings, surveys, interviews, photographs, and many more, but theirs is a supporting role. Without the stories, metrics are meaningless. Consider what ethnographer Paul Stoller writes about what his mentor Songhay sorcerer Adamu Jenitongo once said to him. On a return to Niger, Stoller brought the coauthored manuscript that was eventually to become his acclaimed fieldwork memoir *In Sorcery's Shadow* (Stoller and Olkes, 1987). He translated and read it to his mentor in the evenings over the course of three months. All through that time, his mentor made no comments or corrections. Finally, about to leave for home, Stoller asked "What do you think?" The answer, Stoller writes, changed his life. His mentor said: "You must produce something that will be remembered, something that describes me and you, something that my grandchildren and your grandchildren will use to remember the past, something they will use to learn about the world" (see also Stoller, 2016).

In a letter responding to a student confronting the ethical and emotional demands of a particularly difficult field situation, I wrote: "Listen with your heart, and let their lives flow through you undisturbed, clean and clear, like a ray of light through water. Our commitment is to them, and sharing is part of that commitment." I was trying to convey what I believe to be the fundamental basis of ethnographic research—listening without judging, making a commitment to relationship, giving up the notion of authority and accepting that of responsibility, and finally holding their stories up, seeing the "sense" of them in the context of their and others' histories. That interpretive process requires one to be a bridge, a place with two allegiances, each equally important. Clifford Geertz referred to these two points of identification as Being There and Being Here (1988:130). Few of us could articulate this mediating position as a source of our first field experience unease. I am not sure that it becomes easier when, after many years of experience, we have to negotiate the changes inherent in any organic process.

We are taken by our craft and the discipline of anthropology beyond the retelling of individual stories and even community stories. The stories that we hear are almost never told in obvious ways. They are told in the daily acts of sharing, committing, negotiating, and balancing the idiosyncratic personalities of people with the work of the community. They are told in the rituals surrounding important points in people's lives and in communal celebrations. They are told in the process of finding a place and an identity within larger, impersonal, sometimes hostile contexts. They are told in the many references to the past—the community of memory that acts as a guide for present and future action. They are embedded in the language itself.

CHANGES BROUGHT BY LONG-TERM FIELD RESEARCH

At the 1999 American Anthropological Association meetings, in a session entitled "Passing the Mantle," Elizabeth Colson, then in her fiftieth year of study with the Gwembe Tonga of Zambia, commented on the benefits of long-term field research: "It's a chance of facing my own failures of understanding, and at the same time learning, getting deeper in, and seeing that things are always changing, and therefore that I am living as they are, in the stream of time" (Royce and Kemper 2002:xv).

Ethnographers experience life as it is being lived, see changes as they unfold, and follow particular research themes across generations. We produce "progress reports" of unfolding lives, rather than definitive statements about some particular slice of time in people's lives. We realize our own misperceptions or "failures of understanding," and we generate new questions as we and our hosts change to meet new challenges. Sometimes it is the accumulation of observations and that last piece that allows us to "see" something that may be fundamental to understanding a vital way our hosts have of seeing the world.

For Juchitecos, one of these is acknowledging the distinction between wild (*gui'xhi*) and settled (*guidxhi*). The important piece for me was the taxonomy of flowers, based on where they fit in those two categories. From that, everything formed the underpinning of my understanding of death.

Our ethnographic involvement spans multiple guiding metaphors, paradigmatic shifts, and fashions in funding so we are less likely to "see" with particular and time-delimited blinders. We mature as ethnographers as we work to master the discipline's demands, honing our ability to see and to listen. We work to become good vessels for the lives and stories that flow through us, and we become skilled at crafting ways in which to tell those stories to others who do not know them. One of the highest compliments I have received in my long relationship with the Isthmus Zapotec of Mexico was an inscription a Zapotec writer wrote in a copy of her book that she gave me: "For someone who knows how to listen to my people with the ear of her heart."

CHANGES IN THE ROLE AND PERSON
OF THE ETHNOGRAPHER

Frequent visits over the years, and the commitment of an ethnographer recognized by the people in the community shift the roles of ethnographer and community members. This shift can take many forms. In Juchitán, it means becoming family and being addressed by the appropriate kin terms—sister, daughter, cousin defined my relationship in Delia's family. But there are other terms that are also used. *Na* is applied to an older married woman, though there are exceptions. And as a woman grows older, she becomes part of a category referred to simply as *las tías*—"the aunts." This designation marks someone who is considered wise and as such is a mark of respect that also carries an obligation to care for younger women. I have become part of this collective.

You also find yourself becoming more and more a historian for the community, family, and even individuals. Distant history, yes, because that is part of your preparation and their story, but also recent history of the sort that you personally witnessed and recorded. The year 2017 marked the fiftieth year of my engagement with Juchitán. I have been fortunate because the Juchitecos value each individual's "work" (*dxiiña'*) as it contributes to the community. My work, as both they and I define it, is to listen, understand, and interpret their stories for them and for the world, which has much to learn from them. In December 2016, a third edition of my first book about the community was published—the publisher provided 1,000 copies to be given free to Juchitecos, especially to the youth (Royce, 2016). As I have shared more and more of what I am thinking and writing with them—in the form of talks, photo exhibits, and drafts—they are clearer about the nature and importance of this work. Delia, my Zapotec sister and friend, has read all my work in its draft forms, and frequently remarks to others how full of detail it is. "She remembered all the details of Na Tiquia's funeral—all the kinds of flowers, who came, what was said, how it felt." On one recent trip, a cousin looked at my notebook and commented first on the quality of the book itself, then talked about the craft of observing and recording. I recently wrote a prologue to a book written by a local historian and friend and asked my Zapotec family to read it. "What you said about us and your words were so beautiful, it almost made me cry," said my uncle.

Engaging people in the process of research at all stages has led to collaborations that I could not have imagined at the beginning. People buy copies of new publications for me, save invitations for me to various fiestas (these are often the art work of local painters), make notes of events that might be important for me to know, and keep lists of things for me to see and do on my visits there. They ask me to do television interviews and meet with people who are interested in my work or whose own work might be of interest to me.

My work now is most often collaborative, especially in the arts. My translations of local poet Enedino Jimenez's work were a communal effort, with family and friends sitting around the table arguing about the best way to get from a particular Zapotec phrase to Spanish. My most recent book, *Becoming an Ancestor* (2011), includes the work of many poets in the Zapotec original and my English translations. I had been working on a collaborative project with Zapotec poets, painters, and musicians on the transformative and sustaining roles of the arts, made more prominent by the 2017 8.1 magnitude earthquake. In 2018, I was asked by Indiana University to organize two workshops at the National University of Mexico (UNAM) to celebrate the signing of an agreement between UNAM and Indiana University. In conversations with Zapotec scholars and writers and U.S.-based scholars, we decided to focus on a topic of great importance for Juchiteco writers that is also a fundamental topic for indigenous peoples in general and for scholars who work in these areas. "Voces del Pueblo/El Poder de Palabra e Imágen//Voices of the People/The Power of Word and Image," brought together poets, translators, publishers of indigenous literature and heads of important indigenous organizations representing both Mexico and the United States. We hosted a similar set of workshops, readings, and a film showing in April 2019 at Indiana University.

Writing has been one way of sharing; photography is another. My photographs capture points of memory in the lives of the people of Juchitán. This has been especially true with photographs I have of people now dead. Grandchildren are curious about their ancestors but spouses and siblings cherish these images most. Because a good photograph is essential for the altar in the home that commemorates families who have died, people are eager to have the best one they can find. Often it is one I have taken. In June 2017, the

Casa de la Cultura of Juchitán hosted an exhibit of some of my photos, *Guidxi Stine' Ne Ca Xpanda'/ Mi Pueblo y Sus Retratos*, 1972 to 2015. People came for the next two months—children with parents and grandparents, young people in their twenties. Some came to see themselves and their friends, some to remember friends and family who had died, and some to see what the people and city looked like before they were born.

Technologies change and transform the way we work. Moving from film to digital images means easier access to my photographs for Zapotec friends but it has left me with some 6,000 slides to be digitized so that I can provide the city with a complete digital archive. Fortunately, a state-of-the-art home for the archive may be the one designed and funded by painter Francisco Toledo—a digital archive of photographs of Oaxaca. This will guarantee their preservation and their availability to Juchitecos who would like to see them. Social media like Facebook mean that I am at once connected to virtually everything that is happening and in real time. Smart phones are a useful backup to the heavy professional cameras. And they mean we can message each other any time of the day or night.

Juchitán, more particularly an association of local writers and scholars supported by the Casa de la Cultura (Fundación Histórico Cultural Juchitán) established an award, the Medal of the Zapotec People (Medalla Binniza), to recognize individuals whose work speaks to the history, language, and culture of the Zapotec of the Isthmus of Tehuantepec. In 2016, I became the first non-Zapotec, non-Mexican to be chosen for the award. The awarding of the Medalla Binniza and the simultaneous publication of the third edition of my first book were humbling experiences. The award ceremony and exhibit of a selection of my photographs brought a crowd spanning all ages, family, friends, the local intellectuals who had chosen me for this honor, poets, painters, musicians, photographers, and people from all the sections of the city. It made me realize why this place and these people have been so dear to me for so long. Honoring the very long heritage of the ancestors, appreciating those who support its flowering in all kinds of ways and materials, embracing and mentoring the younger generations, they move fluently in a rapidly globalizing world, practicing that special kind of intimacy and love that embraces difference rather than fearing and annihilating it. They have included me in this work, this *dxiña',* recognizing the uniqueness of my contributions and making it part of the ongoing story of this Isthmus Zapotec city.

BIDO' XHU—EARTHQUAKES

On September 8, 2017, a Thursday evening, an 8.1 magnitude earthquake struck just off the coast of Chiapas and Oaxaca. It was the strongest on record

Figure 4.3   Na Mari, *Totopera* (Maker of *Totopos*), 2010.

since 1932. Of all the towns in Oaxaca, Juchitán de Zaragoza, the second largest city in the state, suffered the most devastation. I could not communicate with my family for almost two days. The city had no electricity, no services at all. I finally succeeded in messaging a niece in Oaxaca City and found that my family was safe though members of the three extended families were all living in the one part of the house that seemed sound.

While Juchitán had faced difficulties before—political problems, flooding, land reform, and the introduction of wind farms among them, this was different—the earthquake left the city physically devastated. Sixty percent of the homes and public buildings in the city were damaged, most rendered uninhabitable. Many families chose to move into the street in case of further tremors. After the second 6.1 quake, my family went to stay with friends whose house had escaped almost intact. Many private and public buildings have since been razed or are scheduled for demolition. These include some of the oldest and most cherished buildings. Two that have since been rebuilt include the Centro Escolar Juchitán, the first large secondary school in the city, brought by the efforts of local hero General Heliodoro Charis Castro and the Chapel of the Fishermen (*Capilla Guzebenda*) a landmark beloved by the inhabitants of the seventh section. The list goes on as inspectors go around the city, surveying and filling out forms, weighing the value as opposed to the cost of reconstruction. Spared and marked for restoration, thanks to experts from the Mexican Instituto Nacional de Antropología e Historia, are the parish church of San Vicente Ferrer, the Casa de la Cultura, and the Palacio Municipal. Juchiteco architect Elvis Jiménez López has begun a project that would rebuild homes based on traditional models, or build new structures that are traditional. The goal is to build in harmony with the landscape, as well as making structures able to withstand future earthquakes. Architect Jiménez López is using early photographs we took as models for both new and rebuilt homes. Local historians have also solicited our early photographs in their documentation of change.

A larger project with national and international reach is that of a documentary film series on Juchitán that focuses on the city before the earthquake and then the subsequent efforts to rebuild. Thus far, there are five 28-minute films in a series on Mexican television Canal 22 titled *El Raíz Doble* (see Appendix). The first, *El sol de movimiento,* uses photographs taken by my husband in 1971–1972 and some of mine from 1974.

Help has come from many places. Cuba sent two fully equipped medical clinics. China sent hundreds of family-sized, heavy rubber tents for temporary housing. Our Latin American and Caribbean Studies program at Indiana University launched a series of fund-raisers, *Pueblo a Pueblo,* for those affected by both the Juchitán earthquakes and the Puerto Rican hurricane. We were able to take advantage of local organizations that have had a history of funding community projects. What has made such an impression on me, however, are all the individual Juchitecos and Juchitecas who know what is essential and possible, and have made them happen. Gubidxa Guerrero and the Comité Melendre created the Adopt an Oven (Adopta un Horno) campaign to replace the big clay pots (*ollas*) that serve as ovens for making *totopos*, a staple of the Isthmus diet and the economic base of many Juchitecas (see Figure 4.3). When they had enough funds to pay the local potters to make the pots for the *totoperas* of Juchitán, they made additional ones to give to the women of smaller, nearby communities. Young poet Elvis Guerra, helping distribute clothing and other goods that came in from distant sources, saw that there was nothing among the donated Western clothes that older Zapotec women would be comfortable wearing. He launched a project for donating cloth, or money to buy cloth, for the long skirts (*enaguas*) and short square blouses (*huipiles*) that are the everyday costume of older women. With leftover funds, he paid Zapotec women to sew the outfits.

These two projects addressed a fundamental need at the same time as they made it possible for people to work again. The first enabled potters to make pots and women to make and sell *totopos*, a basic part of the Juchiteco diet; the second made traditional clothing available and employed local seamstresses. Both allowed people to be economically productive again. My role was helping coordinate local Juchitán projects, matching potential donors with Go-Fund-Me campaigns.

POETS, PAINTERS, MUSICIANS, AND STORYTELLERS

Poets, painters, and musicians have responded to the tragedy of the three earthquakes by helping the most fragile members of the community—the children. They brought children together in workshops, teaching them traditional music, especially the pre-Hispanic Zapotec flute and turtle shell drum. A series of these was offered by young flute player Cosijopi Guisiubi Ahuitzotl, who invited any children who wanted to come: "Everyday, beginning at 5 in the plaza of the fishermen, 7th section, Juchitán, its traditions and its music lives! I cannot offer goods but I do offer my heart and the little that I know" (translation by the author).

Artists in Juchitán and the Galería Gubidxa in the neighboring town of Union Hidalgo, helped children past the shock of losing homes and schools by offering paints, paper, and walls and letting the children find a creative outlet. One of the earliest was making handprints on a wall to say "I am here." Another project, painting Ojos de la Casa ("Eyes of the House") on walls, was designed by Victor Fuentes of Galería Gubidxa, to convince the young painters that, if there are eyes, there will be houses again.

Artist Francisco Ramos donates his time and love of art to children gathered in the seventh section of the city. He gives them paint, brushes, and paper and sets them to painting what they think is important in Juchitán. Poets and writers, all bilingual in Zapotec and Spanish, gather children around in classes and workshops about storytelling, poetry, and learning Zapotec. Established poets such as Irma Pineda, Victor Terán, and Natalia Toledo raise spirits and tell people who they are with their poetry and in readings. Irma Pineda, partnering with the federal institution that publishes works in indigenous languages, invited children to draw pictures of Juchitán, its traditions, and the earthquake. She provided her own poems and the result was a handsome, colorful, illustrated book in Zapotec and Spanish, *Chupa Ladxidua (Dos es mi corazón; "Two is my heart")*. It is available for free as a pdf.

There are also communal activities and gatherings that remind Juchitecos that they have grown and prospered through their actions for the common good. Community kitchens have sprung up in most sections of the city—women cooking food and offering it to those who had lost homes and had no way to feed themselves or their families. The Basic Basket (*canasta básica*) was yet another project in which donated traditional foods were distributed in outlying parts of the city. The food arrived in a colorful straw basket, woven by Juchiteco artisans. It was a generous and culturally appropriate way in which to take the gifts of food, a way to honor the dignity of each person who received the gift. Like the other projects, it also offered employment to the weavers of palm.

Speaking for and with one's home and being heard requires certain beliefs and values. Juchitán's unique ability to support generations of risk-takers and speakers across borders can be found in its long history of acting deliberately to transform itself. That they have been so successful is a testament to their ability to work as a community while respecting each individual member. Community for them is not simply an agglomeration of individuals. It implies a sense of common good while recognizing and respecting individual ways of contributing to it (see Ostrom, 1990). It offers incorporation without demanding the annihilation of unique gifts, yearnings, and culture. Community is dynamic not static, diverse not monolithic, tolerant not judgmental, risk-taking not fearful. The actions of artists, storytellers, community organizers, cooks, and youth who took responsibility for restoring physical and emotional well-being after the earthquake is reason to believe in their power to transform.

FORTY-DAY MASS (MISA DE 40 DÍAS)

"Music and Light will make a flower bloom in the shadows," the poster for the Mass and concert said. In those first forty days I saw hundreds of flowers take root and bloom as Juchitecos of all ages and occupations ministered to each other in ways honored in their language and landscape and values of recognition and reciprocity. The city, the "settled place," has been tossed and torn, moved off its literal foundations but it will bloom again, like the tree of hands with nesting birds on the poster for the forty-day Mass.

The Mass for forty days, the forty days since the first earthquake, was celebrated on October 16 at 6:00 p.m., in the broad street in front of the Municipal Palace. The bishop of the Diocese of Tehuantepec, Monsignor Oscar A. Campos officiated in this ritual of honoring the departed and opening a path of prayer, music, and light for their souls. At the end of the service, more than eighty musicians, including young children, played traditional *sones* to celebrate life and the unity of the Istmeño family. People brought candles that formed a huge cross of light for their departed. They brought other candles that were lit at the beginning of the concert to honor the Juchitán that lives and will be renewed.

My friend, poet Irma Pineda, using a new children's game spawned by the earthquakes, tells us this: "Playing the earthquake game, each child has to play a part: "You will faint," "You will say 'forgive me, God'," "You will die" "Why me? I died the last time!" "It is they with their games and smiles who teach us that we can die more than once, because we are Zapotec [*binnizá*], because we are strong, because we remember that cry in the night of the earthquake, like lightning in the darkness: Rari nuaa, rari' nuudu—I am here, We are here" (Pineda, 2017, translation by the author).

CONFRONTING THE AFTERMATH
OF THE EARTHQUAKES

For me, each of the forty days since the first earthquake brought tears, joy, gratitude, anger, loss, laughter, every emotion colored by an overwhelming sense of the sensibility and strength of this community that had welcomed me fifty years earlier. I followed the successes and frustrations of family and friends from a distance via social media, finding hope in their resilience.

Experiencing the city in May 2018 for the first time since the earthquakes of the previous September, however, was up close and visceral. I pressed my face against the bus window in the early dawn as we approached the hilly town of Matías Romero and began the final descent into the Pacific plains of the Isthmus of Tehuantepec. Everywhere I looked were massive channels scoured into the roadside and fields. Small cantinas were uprooted, and blocks and tiles and pieces of oiled tablecloths scattered across the landscape. The sign advertising a small hotel was all that was left of it. Coming into Juchitán, we bumped over great ruts in the road to the bus station. A pall hung over the city—dust from the rubble and the smell and smoke of exhaust from bulldozers and trucks carrying away remains of houses and businesses. As we drove to my family's house, I saw the empty spaces where homes and businesses of friends had been, the stacks of tiles leaning up against what remained of homes waiting for a time when they could provide a roof again. Nearing the city center, I saw the half that remained of the Municipal Palace. The spacious green central park that had been the Parque Benito Juárez was nowhere visible—it was filled to overflowing with the tents and stands and makeshift *comedores* (little lunch places) of vendors who had lost their shops in the now-collapsed indoor market. Streets were clogged with rubble, new building materials, and workspaces of builders, leaving one narrow lane for all the moto-taxis, cars, contractors' trucks, and buses.

This different experience of the city took me back to earlier years when it was less urban and when there was a lot of green space. On that May visit and a subsequent one in December 2018, I found myself searching out spaces away from the crowded commercial city center on my early morning walks, camera in hand. In front of the family house, the wide spaces with trees and broad streets provided by the smaller park across from the family compound, the neighboring parish church, and the next-door Casa de la Cultura were no longer there. The park was filled with dozens of women food vendors who spilled over from the larger park and who were joined by other opportunistic vendors. The church was closed and a temporary corrugated tin chapel blocked off the wide street just past the family compound. The Casa de la Cultura, another place of calm with its spacious patio, is closed for the foreseeable future.

With all the construction and cordoned-off areas, it was difficult to walk the two blocks to the Foro Ecológico with its botanical garden and broad patios, and then beyond, to the tree-bordered river. So, I found comfort in walking the alleyways (*callejones*) that run from the center out to the further parts of the city. I left the compound early each morning and would choose a different *callejón* to explore. I loved those walks, some through parts of the city that I did not know well. It was early enough that I met vendors on the way to the central market or selling to their customers in the neighborhood. Each greeted me and some, an older woman selling tiny bouquets of wild flowers, engaged me in conversation. I learned the story of an ancient and mammoth Ceiba tree from a woman who lived across the alley from it and whose great grandfather had planted it. When I stopped to photograph a house that was decorated for one of the many May celebrations, I met a man taking advantage of the early morning freshness. In our conversation, it turned out that he knew all about me, had read my first book, and knew my family. In the *callejones* of Cheguigo (the section across the river to the west), everyone greeted me, offered directions or shortcuts or introduced me to their children, or responded to my questions about an interesting bird perched on a wall, which generated a lengthy debate among a family about which was its correct name in Zapotec. I took hundreds of photos of the landscape—long shots down narrow streets, an interesting wrought iron gate (*portón*), and always the stunning murals crafted by artists who wanted to make the city beautiful in the midst of destruction (see Figures 4.4 and 4.5). Some of the views that had enchanted me, I posted to Facebook, and was delighted to see comments from Juchitecos who recognized their neighborhoods.

Part of my difficulty in coming to terms with the post-earthquake city has been that its large commercial center has become even more crowded, commerce taking over all the spaces for sitting and talking or walking or enjoying an ice cream. Some of this is the result of the earthquake that either destroyed the places where people bought and sold, or that took away from

Figure 4.4 "Broken Heart" Mural, 2019.

some the possibilities for earning a living. The result was the expansion of commerce into all the available public spaces, as people try to catch up or get reestablished.

The December trip was an even more exaggerated experience of this. December is a month crammed with Christmas celebrations, weddings, XV birthdays, and two *velas*. Each of these means buying things as gifts or decorations. Commerce expanded to accommodate business, spilling over the boundaries of the Benito Juarez park to line both sides of the main street heading north.

It is difficult to predict how Juchitán will rebuild. Restoring sites considered to be historic treasures will take at least three to five years. The

Figure 4.5 Mural by Suarte Noriega for the Children after the Earthquake, 2018.

indoor market and the Municipal Palace have been rebuilt. There is no overall plan for individually owned structures. Some residents whose homes were destroyed have left the city. Some are unable to recreate the homes they had with the allowances offered by the government. The house of Heliodor Charis is one example. It was deemed too expensive to restore so his daughter has built smaller quarters within the once grand structure. Nonetheless, the economy seems to be regaining much of the ground it lost. The Juchitán-generated campaigns such as those of the Comité Melendre, the generosity of artist Francisco Toledo (born in Juchitán), the workshops of writers and artists, have continued to provide both support and the means for people to get back to work—the *totoperas*, palm weavers, and embroiderers are just three examples. Restaurants and cafes have gradually reopened. The Foro Ecológico, minimally damaged, continues its mission of environmental care-taking and has offered its space to cooperatives and community organizations to continue their work of cultural promotion. The *velas*, those splendid celebrations of community that were not celebrated in that first year after the earthquakes, will once again crowd April and May with Masses, parades, all-night dances, and daytime parties.

RARI NUAA—I AM HERE

In 1967, I had no notion that in 2018, I would still be part of the Zapotec community of Juchitàn, still listening and discovering connections, still photographing the city and its people. I am working with individuals and organizations to rebuild and to help tell their stories locally and globally.

The families with whom I am closest are now in their sixth generation since I first met them. I have witnessed deaths and births, marriages, and moving away. My obligations and responsibilities have become those of a Juchiteca, to individuals and to the community as a whole. They were and are my teachers, my friends, and my family, opening my eyes to a way of living based on community and transformation, on the fundamental importance of relationships, on local commitment and global participation, and of being present to one another. Through the daily work of maintaining family and the work of celebration and commemoration, they craft lives of grace and bountiful offering. In their responses to the devastating 2017 earthquake, we see those values in the remarkable efforts of individuals and the community to rebuild a new Juchitàn.

They have loved me, have helped and formed me as an anthropologist, yes, but more than that, by their pride in being Zapotec and through the example of their actions, they have given me the courage to find my voice, the courage to find joy in unfamiliar paths.

The Zapotec of Juchitán are a remarkable people, surviving all attempts to exterminate or change them. They name and claim themselves in a country and a world that often ignores and certainly undervalues its indigenous people. The community takes pride in its identity because it is an identity that is leading the way rather than being frozen in some Arcadian dreamscape. The Juchitecos say to the world: *rarí' nuudu*—we are here.

APPENDIX

Juchitan: *El Raiz Doble* youtubes, from Canal 22 History and Culture channel. Directed by Mardonio Carballo.

https://www.youtube.com/watch?v=OotxkL8-BBc (*Sol de Movimiento*—includes Anya Peterson Royce and Ronald R. Royce' photographs of the city in the early 1970s)

https://www.youtub.com/watch?v=FOSNjFaGJVU&t=335s (Totoperas)

https://www.youtube.com/watch?v=5bNs9cwJPbU&t=70s (*Colectivo Melendre*)

https://www.youtube.com/watch?v=Vl_v_3JpLvg&t=25s (*Colectivo Binni Biri*)

NOTE

1. To the five generations of Juchitecos, especially the women of my family; to all the poets, artists, musicians, dance partners, and *binni guendabiaani* (wise ones) who have been my teachers, friends, and colleagues. With grace and generosity, they have opened my eyes to a way of living based on community and transformation, and on the fundamental importance of relationships and of being present for

one another. *Diuxquixhepe' laatu.* To my mentor and friend, Elizabeth F. Colson, for her example of long-term ethnography that always held up the voices of her Tongan collaborators. To Ronald R. Royce for the extraordinary photographs he took in 1971–1972, for giving me my first camera, for his profound knowledge of the Zapotec language, and for his insistence that I entertain alternate explanations and listen to many voices. Over the years, he responded to my daily emails from the field, conversations that opened up new ways of seeing and understanding. He was the best of partners.

Chapter 5

Cigarettes, Cash, or Spare Parts

Compensation and Reciprocity in Arctic Research

Edmund (Ned) Searles

"Knowledge and money have no common measure"

(Aristotle, in Simpson 2013:164)

RECIPROCITY AS COMPENSATION

In this chapter, I discuss the challenges of compensating the individuals and families that made my dissertation fieldwork possible.[1] During a nine-month period of ethnographic research in 1994, at a fieldsite located on the eastern edge of the Canadian Arctic, a number of factors made these challenges particularly complicated. It became dramatically clear to me after the first several weeks of my research that my budget was too small to cover my living expenses in Iqaluit and surrounding regions—the location of my fieldwork—and to compensate the research participants who assisted me. This revelation, as well as the budget crisis in which I found myself, sprang from of a series of unanticipated expenses.

The first one occurred two months prior to my arrival in Canada, when I learned that I would have to spend a portion of my research grant to purchase a round-trip ticket from Iqaluit to Seattle. The purpose of this unexpected return trip was to retake one of my graduate school qualifying exams, which I needed to pass in order to proceed to the next phase of my doctoral program—dissertation research and writing. Although my dissertation committee failed me in my first attempt on this exam, they allowed me to retake it, but to do this I needed to return to the University of Washington after only one month in the field.

The second expense occurred a few days before my return trip to Seattle. Seeking research approval, I attended the monthly meeting of the Amaruq Hunters and Trappers Association (AHTA), a local Inuit hunting organization, to present my research plans and field their questions. During the meeting, an AHTA member informed me that I needed to provide my own transportation if I planned to accompany an Inuit family on their hunting excursions. The AHTA did not want Michelle (my fiancée at the time, now wife) and me to be an economic burden to an Inuit family struggling with financial issues of their own, including lacking the money to purchase the equipment and supplies they needed to hunt. If I wanted to investigate the lifeways of an Inuit family dedicated to hunting year-round on a full-time basis—the very goal of my proposed research project—then I needed to buy a snowmobile to make this possible. The next day, I used another large portion of my research grant to purchase a Bravo, the least expensive model for sale at the only Yamaha dealer within a 1,000 miles (the nearest major city was Montreal, a three-hour flight away).

Michelle and I encountered a third unexpected expense when we returned to Iqaluit from Seattle. Reveling in the good news that I passed my qualifying exam and could now resume my dissertation research, I disembarked the plane at the Iqaluit airport optimistic about my future in anthropology. As we stepped out of the taxi that drove Michelle and me to our home base at the Iqaluit Research Centre (now the Nunavut Research Institute), the manager invited us in her office for a meeting. She informed us that we were no longer allowed to stay in the Research Centre for free, a benefit that accompanied our permit to conduct ethnographic research in the Northwest Territories of Canada in early January. Beginning the next day, we would have to pay $60 a night to stay there, an expense I had not included in my original research budget.

Overwhelmed by so many unforeseen expenses and anxious about how I was going to afford to live at my fieldsite, much less compensate research participants for their time and knowledge, I thought that a visit to an Inuit friend's house to watch a Hollywood film might lift my spirits. When Michelle and I arrived at Jamasee's house, a fifteen-minute walk from the Research Centre, I was surprised to learn that his adoptive parents were the elderly Inuit couple whom I had recently seen being interviewed on television about their knowledge of Inuit life prior to contact with *Qallunaat* ("white people" in Inuktitut, the official language of Inuit). To our delight, the couple was eager to share some of their knowledge with us, as well. Aqaaqa, Jamasee's father, began recounting an early childhood memory. Realizing that we were unable to understand him (Jamasee's parents were monolingual Inuktitut speakers), Jamasee's forty-year-old brother, Markoosie, began translating for us his father's words. Both the story and the translation made me feel like my research was finally progressing. As Aqaaqa finished his story, the room grew silent. Breaking the silence, Markoosie told us that he could translate more of his father's stories for $50 an hour, a rate that seemed high to me at the time but which I later learned was a competitive rate among local translators. Markoosie was eager to move into his own place but had been unable to find steady employment since he returned to Iqaluit several months previously after completing a prison sentence. Realizing that I would be obliged to pay him if his father began telling another story, I signaled to Michelle that it was time for us to leave. As we pulled on our boots and zipped up our parkas, we thanked Aqaaqa, his wife, and their sons for their hospitality. Closing the door behind us, Michelle and I turned to face a relentless northwest wind. Walking back to the Research Centre through the dark, empty streets of Iqaluit, the wind stinging our cheeks, I wondered if the dream of becoming a professional anthropologist was beyond my reach: if one story was beyond my price range, how could I afford to collect enough for an entire dissertation?

Determined to find a way to move forward, I called an Inuit friend and asked him if he knew of a family in town with a spare room and who could take in a young *Qallunaat* couple. He told me to call his sister-in-law, Mary Ellen. She and her Inuit husband, Udlu, owned a three-bedroom house located a short distance from the Research Centre. To my delight, Mary Ellen invited us to move in with her husband and children right away, informing us that we could have the spare bedroom, which her husband was using to store boat and snowmobile motors in need of repair. When I inquired about rent, Mary Ellen said that while we did not need to pay, we could help with household chores, including cooking, cleaning, and caring for their three school-aged children.

Through this new arrangement of participating in an Inuit household, Michelle and I began to learn the Inuit rules of reciprocity. Contributing our skills, time, knowledge, and supplies to an Inuit family entitled us to "free" shelter and food. We became enmeshed in a system of shared resources and labor known as *ningiqtuq*, a family-based structure that integrates individual households into larger extended family networks or *ilagiit* (Wenzel, 1995). In this way, we experienced firsthand the *ningiqtuq* of Mary Ellen's *ilagiit*, which included, in addition to her nuclear family, her husband's father and his five adult children and their spouses and children. The *ningiqtuq* structured and regulated the sharing of basic needs, including food, shelter, supplies, and hunting equipment within and across several different households. Although family members did not demand cash payment for rent, they expected us to share whatever we owned or earned with other family members, including our time, knowledge, resources, and pocket money. The Bravo snowmobile I purchased to satisfy the demands of the Hunters and Trappers Association became a collectively owned resource available to any *ilagiit* member who

wanted to use it. With the money I received from future research grant install-
ments, I purchased fuel and spare parts for the Bravo in addition to other
goods and items that *ilagiit* members demanded, including large quantities of
"junks" (e.g., candy bars, chips, and soda) and cigarettes.

In what follows, I explore how the local rules of reciprocity guided the
ways in which Inuit—as well as two novice anthropologists—related to and
depended on each other daily for social and moral support. I argue that learning and following the Inuit rules of reciprocity became a culturally specific
means of compensating the Inuit family members who assisted me with my
research. I also reflect on the various models of compensation described by
Arctic anthropologists and examine why exposing the intricate details of
compensating research participants is taboo. This taboo is upheld, at least in
part, I suggest, by anthropologists' reluctance to acknowledge the power gap
between researcher and "subjects" that compensation inevitably creates and
that reciprocity is designed to address. Finally, I discuss some of the many
challenges that local rules of reciprocity pose for ethnographers, entangling
them in complicated—sometimes distressing—dramas that result from family members' competing demands. Even though ethnographers might fall
short of upholding the rules of reciprocity, such shortcomings often yield
tremendous anthropological insights about the ways in which people relate to
one other and make sense of the world around them. Before I discuss those
details, however, a brief description of the particular world that informed my
own research is in order.

"OUR LAND"

Nunavut ("our land" in Inuktitut) has a population of approximately 36,000
inhabitants, 85 percent of whom self-identify as Inuit (Statistics Canada,
2017). Iqaluit, a town with as many *Qallunaat* (non-Inuit or "white people")
residents as Inuit, is home to several of the Inuit families with whom I lived
during my dissertation research in 1994 and 1996 (see Figure 5.1). It is also
the capital of Nunavut and Baffin Island's largest town.

At the time of my fieldwork, Nunavut was still in the planning stages. The
region where I conducted my research was part of the Northwest Territories
of Canada. Beginning in the early 1990s, Inuit leaders and federal negotiators
devised a plan to divide the territory in half. The western half would remain
the Northwest Territories and the eastern half would become Nunavut.[2] As
its name suggests, Nunavut became the first territory in Canada with a majority indigenous population. In creating an indigenous-dominated territory,
Nunavut's architects hoped this new government would transform the settler-
dominated status quo, shifting economic and political power from a small,
elite group of *Qallunaat* entrepreneurs to Inuit individuals and organizations.

Figure 5.1 Iqaluit, 2018.

The plan also established more ethically rigorous guidelines for research involving indigenous populations. Not only would researchers have to explain how their work would contribute new knowledge to their disciplines, but they would also have to articulate how it would benefit Nunavut Inuit individuals and society, more generally. This required researchers to begin decolonizing their research methods by integrating opportunities for collaboration and cooperation with indigenous participants and securing funds for compensating them that had been previously absent from research budgets.

The set of principles used to guide the operation of the Nunavut government became known as *Inuit Qaujimajatuqangit* ("that which Inuit have known since long ago") or IQ for short. Following a series of workshops and interviews involving Inuit elders in the 1980s, IQ become codified into eight guiding principles (see Karetak et al., 2017). These principles were based on how Inuit organized their communities, socialized youth, managed conflict, and lived communally prior to the arrival of permanent White settler populations in the late 1800s and early 1900s. In recent years, IQ has become much more than a blueprint for running a government. As Karetak et al. (2017:3) write: "It is an ethical framework and detailed plan for having a good life . . . key among [this] is *inunnguiniq*, the making of a human being."

Inuit personhood involves maintaining strong ties to the natural environment through hunting and foraging, as well as other traditional subsistence activities, such as making skin-clothing and building a snow house (*iglu*). Maintaining ties to the natural environment has become increasingly difficult for many reasons, and some of those are due to federal regulations and cultural taboos that prevent Inuit from selling "country food," or food obtained locally through hunting, fishing, and foraging (see Gombay 2009, 2010; Harder and Wenzel, 2012; Kishigami, 2000; Ready and Power, 2018; Searles, 2016; Wenzel, 1991). Many Inuit argue that selling country food threatens the viability of traditional culture by undermining local rules of reciprocity that are sustained by non-monetary exchanges of goods and labor (Balikci, 1964; Graburn, 1969; Harder and Wenzel, 2012; Nuttall et al., 2005; Wenzel, 2013). Food and clothing obtained and/or made from locally caught animals belong to the *ilagiit*, not to individual Inuit. Individual *ilagiit* members are also obligated to help other family members when hunting large game, such as whales and walrus, which requires several boats and strong bodies working together in unison. The free flow and sharing of goods and labor within the *ilagiit* is a key adaptive feature of the contemporary subsistence economy (Wenzel, 2000).

Inuit contrast the subsistence economy, which they view as authentically Inuit, with the cash economy, which they associate with *Qallunaat* culture and values. Whereas the cash economy treats labor and goods as commodities whose prices are determined by impersonal market forces, the subsistence economy considers labor and goods, such as country food, as forms of credit that hunted animals bestow upon hunters. As Mark Nuttall (2000:54–5) explains:

> Free distribution of meat from seals and other marine mammals is an acknowledgement of the debt owed to the animal coming to the hunter and a denial that any one person has exclusive claims to ownership of the animals that are caught . . . Cultural identity is founded upon and derives meaning from a culturally embedded system of shared relations.

Not surprisingly, attempts to mix the cash and subsistence economies by creating markets for the sale of country food in the Arctic are often controversial (see Searles, 2016). In addition, the cultural and social capital associated with obtaining and sharing country food is very high, a point I learned in my 1994 fieldwork. Not only do Inuit consider country food healthier and more nutritious than *Qallunaat* food (food produced and packaged outside the Arctic and purchased in stores), but many contend that learning how to obtain, prepare, and share country food are key to being Inuit (Searles 2002, 2016; see also Searles, 2010).

The social stigma associated with selling country food, combined with low prices for animal skins have made it difficult, if not impossible, for

Inuit to make money from hunting. Consequently, hunters are dependent on family members and the government for support (Wenzel, 2000). This was particularly true for Inuit families who lived in *nunaligaalait* ("outpost camps"), where they hunted full-time. *Nunaligaalait* were year-round settlements consisting of one or two households belonging to the same *ilagiit*. They were established in the early 1960s at the time when the vast majority of Inuit began to settle permanently in *nunaliit* ("government-built towns"). Hoping to address the problem of overcrowding caused by a housing shortage, government officials offered Inuit families grants and loans to return to the sites where their parents and grandparents had lived prior to moving to towns like Iqaluit. These outpost camps benefitted from the financial support of regional government agencies and Inuit organizations, such as the Hunters and Trappers Association.

In the mid-1990s, there were six active outpost camps along the coastline of Frobisher Bay in southern Baffin Island, and one of my principal research topics at the time was how these outpost camps managed to preserve a way of life that most other Inuit had abandoned decades ago (see Figure 5.2). Although outpost camp residents were poor by *Qallunaat* standards, they were rich by Inuit ones. This was because residents were able to regularly catch and distribute thousands of pounds of highly valued country food,

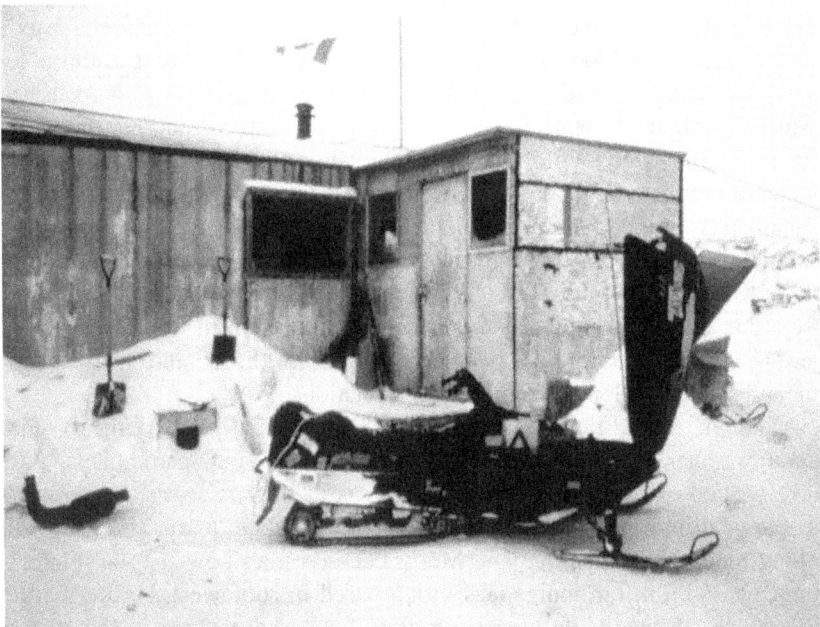

Figure 5.2   Kuyait Outpost Camp, 1994.

including the meat of walrus, caribou, bearded seal, ringed seal, and Canada goose, as well eider duck eggs and Arctic char. Through their efforts, they produced large quantities of country food for town-based family members who did not have the time, knowledge, or resources to hunt. These family members reciprocated by providing financially struggling hunters spare parts for their snowmobiles, hunting supplies, and cigarettes. Throughout my field-work, I observed how Inuit rules of reciprocity informed local people's acts of sharing and exchange. Not only did my observations highlight the cultural importance of these rules, but they also exposed the potential problems asso-ciated with other forms of exchange, such as purchasing country food from a hunter with cash. Although this transaction was acceptable between an Inuit hunter and his *Qallunaat* neighbor, it was unacceptable between Inuit, espe-cially among family members. In fact, demanding cash for food or labor from a family member always had the potential to contaminate, even desecrate, the local rules of reciprocity that kept food, equipment, and labor flowing freely between members of the same *ilaagit*.

AN UNSPOKEN TABOO

Shifting to the examination of another set of rules, namely the rules of rep-resentation in anthropological discourse, Lisa Stevenson states that writing about paying research collaborators and informants is one of anthropology's unspoken taboos (2006:9). This is certainly true of most Arctic anthropolo-gists, who tend to avoid discussing, at least in print, how they compensated their research participants. This omission seems odd, considering the asser-tion made by one group of researchers (Dutheil et al. 2015:149) that monetary compensation is a key feature of all field-based research relationships in the Canadian Arctic. Perhaps this omission is due to the fact that anthropologists often assume the role of a family member in fieldwork contexts (Briggs, 1986; Kan, 2001; Straus, 2001), in which case paying one's "family" is inap-propriate, even insulting. Open and honest discussion of the intricacies of various compensation models would be helpful for those interested in build-ing and sustaining long-term field-based relationships.

Although Arctic anthropologists have been generally unwilling to write about whether and how much they pay their research participants, they have written extensively about other aspects of their relationships with the people who informed their research. In an article about her partnership with a long-time research participant, Molly Lee describes how she met Flora, a renowned Yup'ik (an indigenous group based in southwest Alaska) basket weaver, by chance while harvesting grass for basket-making in the coastal Alaskan village of Platinum. After traveling to dozens of towns in rural

Alaska with Flora over a period of eight years, Lee (2006:33) realized: "I have been engaged all along in a double project. My study of Yup'ik basketry is inextricably tied to the growth of a cross-cultural friendship, and the friendship has molded the form this study has assumed."

After dedicating many decades of fieldwork with a neighboring group of Yup'ik, Ann Fienup-Riordan (2000:186) describes how gifts of food and names shaped her long-term relationships with several Yup'ik families on Nelson Island:

> When I first arrived on Nelson Island in the early 1970s, people gave me two things repeatedly—food and names. The food usually took the form of cooked soup or dried fish shared at the kitchen table. This meant acceptance as well as a full stomach, as I had little money and no skills or equipment to catch my dinner. Later, when I got my own small house, gifts included fresh meat or fish for me to cook and share in my turn with those eating at my table. Over the years friends mark my comings and goings with gifts of fish, berries, and birds.

The gift of names bestowed upon Fienup-Riordan, her husband, and her children reveal a set of nuanced Yup'ik ideas about culture, morality, and personhood (see also McElroy, 2008).

One anthropologist who breached the taboo on monetary compensation was (the late) Steven McNabb, an anthropologist who justified his use of cash to compensate his research participants in a commentary he wrote for an academic journal in 1993. Prior to his death in 1995, McNabb belonged to an expanding cohort of academically trained anthropologists turned professional consultants for various indigenous and nonindigenous organizations in Alaska and Canada. These organizations contracted anthropologists to conduct social science research, creating a new research culture in which anthropologists combined administrative responsibilities with ethnographic research methods (see also Dyck and Waldram, 1993; Freeman, 1973; Usher, 1993). According to McNabb (1993:217), this new era transformed indigenous knowledge and labor into commodities for which anthropologists were obligated to pay:

> We no longer live in that simpler world (if it ever existed) in which we assume a benign reciprocity between generous native and grateful investigator. In the current sociopolitical context, that attitude merely sustains an unequal balance of dependency that favors the researcher. We wouldn't dream of paying for a taxi ride with a smile and a thank you; if the world of research has in fact become commoditized (and it has), then a failure to extend those benefits of that industry to all participants seems little more than exploitation of the most powerless group which, paradoxically, is the source of the commodity.

Not only does McNabb consider not paying one's research participants unethical, but his model leaves no room for the possibility of field-based relationships in which money is only part of the equation, including ones based on a friendship and/or partnership.

Attempting to balance the demands of ethnographic fieldwork with the aspirations of indigenous groups, anthropologists are now developing formal partnerships with local indigenous individuals and organizations. Carol Jolles, who began her anthropological career investigating the roles of faith, food, and family in the lives of Yup'ik residents of St. Lawrence Island (see Jolles, 2002), later partnered with community elders in several Yup'ik villages, a regional school district, and an indigenous scholar to codirect a study of the history of whaling in the Bering Strait region. Jolles (2006:52) claims that "projects that depend on cooperative working relationships with native communities or that shift perspective and primary responsibility from western scholars to indigenous scholars" are ethically imperative. Although Jolles emphasizes that her project received enthusiastic support from the local community, she does not discuss the issue of monetary compensation. Aside from mentioning how the project leaders had to "refuel" groups of Yup'ik interns involved in the research with "necessary soda and chips" (Jolles 2006:49) to keep them focused, Jolles does not explain if or how much researchers paid local people to participate in the project and how such payment might have impacted the relationships that developed between researchers and research subjects.

Working with a research model similar to Jolles's, Michael Kral teamed with Inuit scholar Lori Idlout to direct a multi-community study of the causes and consequences of the suicide epidemic in Nunavut in the early 2000s. Their study relied entirely on community cooperation and collaboration in all phases of the research, from initial design to final product, a model they refer to as participatory action research. Although they do not discuss the role of money in soliciting collaborators and research participants, they mention that in the end the project cost "much in time, resources, and even personal funds" (Minore, quoted in Kral and Idlout 2006:67), and that they even ran out of money at one point. Like Jolles, Kral and Idlout do not discuss how the issue of monetary compensation might have affected the relationships that developed between them and members of the community-based research teams.

Unlike most anthropologists, who avoid the topic of compensation in their published works, Jean Briggs openly discussed the challenges and dilemmas of compensation, even making them front and center in her book. In *Never in Anger* (1970), Briggs provided vivid details of how desire for access to and even control of her cache of "kapluna" ("Qallunaat" or "white people") resources, including tobacco, sugar, flour, and tea, affected her relationships with her research participants, the *Utkuhikhalingmiut* ("Utku" for short), an

Inuit community consisting of 20 to 35 individuals living 150 miles south of the nearest town of Gjoa Haven. She explained (1970:227) that all of the Utku who visited her or helped her with a task—whether lighting a frozen camp stove, erecting a tent, or moving supplies from one camping spot to the next—expected to be compensated with a share of her supplies. Negotiating access to her supplies was a major theme of Briggs's description of her relationship with her host father, Inuttiaq, and "grandfather," Pala. She wrote (1970:243) that their desire for her tobacco, which as a non-smoker she did not use herself, was a considerable source of tension throughout her fieldwork.

The book's detailed descriptions reveal to readers just how much Briggs learned about Utku culture through her daily struggles with trying to distribute her supplies fairly and equitably among research participants. Briggs also wrote at length about the many ways in which she depended on her hosts for food, shelter, and safety. Through the regular, albeit anxiety-inducing acts of exchanging goods, labor, and knowledge, Briggs learned the Utku rules of reciprocity. Acknowledging her dependence on her Utku hosts for her very survival and well-being, while also acknowledging that their use of her kapluna supplies strained her relationships with them, Briggs demonstrated that the taboo on addressing the details of compensation during fieldwork might actually disadvantage students of anthropology. Revealing both the positive and negative sides of anthropologists' relationships with their research participants, and reflecting on their mistakes, anxieties, and imperfections in handling these relationships can provide students and general readers with more honest, balanced, and nuanced ethnographic portraits of the people whom anthropologists study.

GOOD BROTHER, BAD BROTHER

Like Jean Briggs's experience among the Utku, Michelle and I also became integrated into an Inuit family network (*ilaagit*) as we became dependent on its members for food, safety, and survival, especially when traveling to and from Kuyait—the family's outpost camp located 200 miles from Iqaluit—and when hunting in surrounding areas. Also similar to Briggs's situation, we had to contend with numerous episodes in which one or both of us failed at being the kind of child or sibling our Inuit hosts expected us to be.

This was particularly true when Michelle and I had to choose which branch of the *ilaagit* to stay with during the break-up period, which happens every summer in Frobisher Bay. With rare exceptions, nearly all of this massive body of saltwater freezes solid in late December or early January, making it possible to travel around the hundreds of miles of coastline by snowmobile or dog team. In summer when most of the ice melts, one can also travel easily by boat in open water. In the period between solid sea ice and open water, however, is break-up, a time when large sections of sea ice fragment into smaller pieces that eventually melt or are pushed out into the Labrador Sea by wind and tides. During break-up, there is too little sea ice to travel by snowmobile, but there is too much for boating. The only safe option is to remain in place—either in town or at an outpost camp—until the ice melts or clears out of the Bay.

In June 1994, our host brother, Ooleetoa, had planned to spend the break-up period with his father and brother at Kuyait, the family's outpost camp. Michelle and I had just spent part of April and most of May at Kuyait, where we were participating in the camp's daily routines of hunting and fishing. During a brief return trip to Iqaluit with Ooleetoa, Michelle learned that she was accepted into the University of Illinois's doctoral program in anthropology and would begin classes in late August. She needed to return to Seattle in late July in order to move our belongings from Washington State to Illinois and find an apartment in Champaign. We decided that it would be too risky to return to Kuyait with Ooleetoa; if break-up happened, Michelle would be stranded there until August or even later, when we could travel to Iqaluit by boat.

Although we decided to remain with Ooleetoa's brother's family in town, we still had not decided who would retain use of the Bravo snowmobile. As part of my commitment to being a good son and brother, I transferred control of the Bravo to the *ilagiit*. This meant that any member of the family who needed it could borrow it on demand. Ooleetoa used it most frequently, since he was often the only person in the family without access to a snowmobile. This was particularly true when he was staying in Iqaluit, where other members had their own snowmobile or car.

Ooleetoa's appropriation of the snowmobile was actually convenient for Michelle and me, as he was willing to take us anywhere we needed to go (see Figure 5.3). He was an excellent handler: skilled and fearless, yet careful. I had no experience driving a snowmobile, and I knew I would get hopelessly lost if I tried to travel beyond the limits of Iqaluit on my own. I was dependent on someone with advanced navigational and driving skills to transport Michelle and me safely to my various research locations, including Kuyait and surrounding hunting and fishing sites. Ooleetoa became that someone. I had first met him four years previously when I was in Baffin Island for a month as a member of a team of archaeologists and scientists; he was the younger brother of Pauloosie, one of the Inuit men hired by our team, and the brother-in-law of Mary Ellen, our host sister/mother in Iqaluit.[3]

Ooleetoa's geographical knowledge of southern Baffin Island was advanced far beyond that of his peers in Iqaluit. His parents took him out of school after he completed third grade to raise him at the Kuyait outpost

Figure 5.3   Ooleetoa with the Yamaha Bravo, 1994.

camp. While his classmates in town were memorizing multiplication tables, Ooleetoa was learning to find his way in a blinding blizzard, detect the subtle shade differences between safe and "rotten" (dangerous) sea ice, and butcher a seal.

As his brother and apprentice during the winter months of 1994, I experienced firsthand the impressive depth and breadth of Ooleetoa's geographical knowledge and his extraordinary hunting abilities. Not only could he tirelessly navigate the snowmobile through jagged fields of rough sea ice or fearlessly drive straight up and down steep embankments, but he could find his way in the dark, as well. Traveling during the prolonged darkness of Arctic winter days was never a challenge for him, even though the Bravo's headlight was only strong enough to illuminate a path 10 feet ahead.

As Ooleetoa was preparing to make the journey to Kuyait by snowmobile in early June with his father, he assumed that he would drive the Bravo alongside his father's snowmobile, even though he knew that he would not be towing Michelle and me behind on the sled, as he usually did. The problem, however, was that Ooleetoa's older brother, Udlu—Mary Ellen's husband and our housemate—also wanted access to the snowmobile in Iqaluit during the break-up period. Unable to repair his snowmobile's broken engine, Udlu wanted to use the Bravo to take his children, Michelle, and me to his favorite hunting and fishing spots near Iqaluit. Unlike Ooleetoa, who was young and single and thus free to travel as he pleased, Udlu had family responsibilities;

he needed to stay in Iqaluit to help care for his children, who would not be out of school for several weeks.

According to the local rules of reciprocity, both Ooleetoa and Udlu were entitled to borrow the snowmobile as they were both members of the *ilaagit*. I also learned that as the person who purchased the snowmobile, I had the deciding vote in the decision. In the end, I informed Ooleetoa that the Bravo would remain in Iqaluit during break-up. While I imagined that my decision might disappoint him, I did not expect him to be so angry. He accused me of putting his father and him at risk during their journey to Kuyait. For their own safety, they needed two snowmobiles in case one of them broke down or got submerged traveling over rotten ice.

Several days later, I talked to Ooleetoa by two-way radio. I learned that his journey to Kuyait had, thankfully, been an easy one. He seemed very content to be at camp, as well, even without access to the Bravo. He told me that he and his father were repairing the storage shed next to the house; in their absence, a polar bear had broken in to steal some frozen meat and had damaged the roof.

As this dramatic encounter reveals, following the local rules of reciprocity is not easy or straightforward, and the consequences are not always positive. Sometimes they entail pleasing one family member while frustrating another. Two weeks after my confrontation with Ooleetoa, Michelle left for Seattle, boarding her first flight from Iqaluit to Montreal. A few days later, Mary Ellen informed me that she and Udlu had just had a difficult conversation. He informed her that he was no longer comfortable with me living in the spare bedroom, and that either I needed to find another place to live or he would. Perhaps I had done something to upset him, or maybe he was uncomfortable with me as a single man living in his house after Michelle's departure. Maybe it was a combination of both factors. I will never know for sure, since cultural norms prevented me from directly asking him why. Nonetheless, I began looking for another place to stay.

As the ancient Daoist proverb states, "It is upon bad fortune that good fortune leans" (Zhang 2014:159). Indeed, shortly after my bad fortune of losing a place to stay, a neighbor informed me that I could move into her friend's apartment, which was located just a short distance from Mary Ellen and Udlu's house. Her friend was traveling the next day to Pangnirtung, a town located approximately 500 miles north of Iqaluit, to visit her parents and siblings for several weeks. She wanted someone to stay in her apartment while she was away, and this arrangement worked out perfectly.

A week after I moved out of his house, Udlu's desire for distance from me seemed to have dissipated. He called me by phone and invited me to join him on a camping trip to Drafty Mansions, a popular fishing and camping spot approximately 20 miles from Iqaluit. Udlu was confident that the sea

Figure 5.4   Pauloosie, Udlu's Younger Brother, Rolling a Cigarette, 1994.

ice would remain strong enough for the next couple of weeks to support a snowmobile, and he wanted to take advantage of this. Toward the end of our phone conversation, I asked him if the Bravo needed any spare parts or if I could purchase anything else for the trip. "A few spark plugs and a spare track," he responded. "Oh, and a pack of Players Lights [his favorite brand of cigarettes]," he added (see Figure 5.4).

Three months after our successful trip to Drafty Mansions, I began preparing for my departure from the field. With my visa expiring at the end of September, I felt ready to join Michelle in Illinois and begin writing my dissertation. I was also completely out of research money; in fact, I had gone into considerable debt. Although I wanted to give the Bravo to Udlu's family as a departing gift, that would have left me with no money to help Michelle with the security deposit and first month of rent for our new apartment in Champaign. After discussing the matter with Mary Ellen, she told me that given the circumstances, it was culturally acceptable to sell the Bravo to Udlu's father, the head of the *ilagiit*. In the end, I offered to sell it to him for $1,500, $3,000 less than I paid for it eight months previously. He enthusiastically accepted my offer. Although I will never be able to reciprocate the debt I owed him and his children for taking care of Michelle and me during our time at Kuyait and in Iqaluit, keeping us safe through all sorts of perilous situations (including me, falling through the sea ice), and teaching me so much about life in the Arctic, I did my best to share what I could. Given his willingness to purchase the snowmobile, I am confident that he understood my situation. Although I was his "son," I was also a financially insecure graduate student who would soon be getting married and would have many bills to pay in *Qallunaani*, the land of the *Qallunaat*.

CONCLUSION

A series of unanticipated research expenses forced me to become dependent on an *ilagiit*—an Inuit extended family—for food, shelter, and safety during my 1994 fieldwork in southern Baffin Island. Instead of paying our host family rent for allowing my fiancée and me to stay in their house in Iqaluit, I used a third of my research grant to purchase a new snowmobile, which became common property for several households. With the remainder of my research grant, I purchased spare parts for the snowmobile as well as hunting supplies and cigarettes, which I shared with family members, especially those whom we accompanied to the Kuyait outpost camp, a day's journey by snowmobile from Iqaluit. In learning to negotiate what was expected of us and what we were entitled to as members of the *ilagiit*, Michelle and I learned the Inuit rules of reciprocity, which dictate that family members share their money, goods, and labor with the extended family. Learning and following these local rules provided me with my most important lessons about Inuit culture.

Despite an extensive anthropological literature on Canadian Inuit culture, anthropologists are surprisingly silent on a key component of long-term ethnographic research, namely the processes by which anthropologists compensate their research participants. Two notable exceptions are Steven McNabb, who argued that researchers should pay their participants for their knowledge, and Jean Briggs, who carefully detailed how sharing—and not sharing—her cache of *Qallunaat* ("white people") supplies profoundly affected her relations with her Utku host family (Briggs, 1970). Following McNabb and Briggs, I have revealed here the challenges I faced in learning how to compensate my research participants and how my attempts at doing so—contributing to a collectively owned and managed pool of money, hunting equipment, and labor—affected my relationships with my research participants and influenced my research findings.

When I returned to Iqaluit in Spring 2014 to conduct research on the rising rates of food insecurity in the Canadian Arctic, I was no longer a graduate student but rather a recently tenured associate professor of anthropology at Bucknell University. After spending a day volunteering at a local soup kitchen, helping to prepare and serve hundreds of meals to food-insecure residents of Iqaluit, most of whom were Inuit, I went to visit Meeka, an Inuit friend who invited me to join her and her daughter for a dinner of boiled seal meat and frozen Arctic char. As I approached their neighborhood, I suddenly recognized the location; it was not far from the house in which twenty years previously I had listened to Aqaaqa recount a story from his childhood. I also remembered that, following the story, his son Markoosie had asked me if I was willing to pay him $50 an hour to translate more of his father's stories.

Feeling full and happy after a meal of seal meat, I poured myself a cup of tea and sat on the couch near Meeka, who was scrolling through photographs on her laptop. She began showing me images of the Inuit elders and organizations for whom she had been working for the past five years, documenting detailed knowledge of the behavior patterns of the animals that Inuit have hunted for generations. She told me about a new research project she was hoping to start in the next few years, a multiyear survey of the traditional environmental knowledge of those same Inuit elders who, like her parents and grandparents, grew up before the establishment of Qallunaat-controlled towns and institutions.

"How much do you need?" I asked.

"About five million dollars," she answered, "which includes daily per diems for all of the elders involved in the study, as well as the cost of traveling with them to historic sites and translating the interviews."

Although I should have been surprised by this amount, which was considerably more money that I had to conduct my entire dissertation research in the mid-1990s, it actually seemed reasonable to me. Working as a postdoctoral fellow at Université Laval in Québec, Canada for three years prior to obtaining a faculty position in the United States, I worked on a multimillion dollar grant application that was awarded to an international team of social scientists, who were partnering with indigenous organizations to conduct the first-ever multinational survey of living conditions of indigenous peoples in the Circumpolar North. I was disheartened, however, by how far away that research world seemed from me now. I have not applied for a major research grant of my own since I was a graduate student. Applying for and obtaining a research grant of that magnitude would require me to seriously rethink—or, at the very least, taking a leave of absence from—my current position as a professor and department chair at an undergraduate liberal arts university. Teaching and service to my university have become my primary responsibilities, and research, while still important and valued, is limited to what I can accomplish in the summer months or in my "free" time during the academic year when I am not preparing for classes, grading piles of student papers, responding to dozens of emails, planning department meetings, and writing scores of letters of support for colleagues and students alike. And then there are the responsibilities associated with my roles within my own (non-fieldwork) families, as a father, son, brother, spouse, and in-law.

Although still daunted by the enormous size of Arctic research budgets, I am heartened by the fact that I am still able to conduct ethnographic research in the Canadian Arctic on a much smaller scale. I am also grateful for the support that indigenous researchers like Meeka and Nunavut residents like Mary Ellen Thomas (my former host sister/mother) gave, who continue to support my research with free meals, conversation, and companionship whenever I am in Iqaluit. I am able to visit them every several years thanks to generous research support provided by university. My university's competitive International Research Travel Grant covers the cost of round-trip transportation from Lewisburg to Iqaluit, as well as a week's worth of lodging, but not much more than that. Although part of me longs to participate in massive projects like the one proposed by Meeka, another part of me has accepted that given my work/life situation, these are beyond my reach, at least for now.

Reflecting on my own fieldwork over the past thirty years, learning how to conduct Arctic research on a limited budget has forced me to be creative and flexible in ways I never imagined. During my dissertation fieldwork, working without enough money to pay for food, lodging, and interviews provided me the opportunity to learn and follow the Inuit rules of reciprocity in order to survive. It also provided me an important window into Inuit culture, teaching me how Inuit learn about, contribute to, and rely on extended family networks in times of material scarcity, adaptive strategies that they developed long before they became entangled in global capitalism. I encourage future researchers to be not only flexible and creative in the field, but to be more willing to write about how they compensate their research participants and what they learn through that process. Indeed, anthropologists have much to learn from one another about the challenges of compensating those with whom we work in ethical, nonexploitative, and culturally appropriate and meaningful ways.

NOTES

1. Acknowledgments: This is a revised and expanded version of the paper I first presented at the 2017 Annual Meetings of the Society for Applied Anthropology on the panel, "Trails of Reciprocity: Compensation, Friendship, and Helping in Fieldwork Encounters" organized by Michelle Johnson. I thank her for the invitation to participate in it. I am also grateful for her helpful comments and meticulous copy editing on earlier drafts of my chapter. I am also grateful for the insightful comments from Alma Gottlieb and one anonymous reviewer. The research that informed this chapter was funded by grants from the University of Washington, the Foundation for Educational Exchange between Canada and the United States of America Fulbright Program, the National Science Foundation, and the International Association of

Canadian Studies. I would like to thank the Baffin Regional Inuit Association and the Science Institute of the Northwest Territories for exemptions and permits that made my fieldwork possible. Finally, I am forever indebted to the Pisuktie-Thomas family, who kept Michelle and me safe and sane during our first stay in southern Baffin Island in 1994 and who continue to support us whenever we need it.

2. April 1, 1999 is the official birth date of Nunavut.

3. Mary Ellen was both our host "mother" and a host "sister." Within the ilagiit, she was structurally a sister, as she was the daughter-in-law of Aksujuleak, the head of the Kuyait outpost camp. He referred to Michelle as *paniga* ("my daughter"), and by extension, I was his *irniq* ("son"). When we stayed with Mary Ellen in her home in Iqaluit, she was more of a mother than a sister to us, due to the simple fact that we were more like her children than her siblings-in-law. We lacked the skills and knowledge typical of other adults in our age cohort, an experience described by many anthropologists (for a detailed example, see Briggs 1986).

Chapter 6

Conversations and Critiques on Creating an Anthropological "Family"

Chelsea Wentworth and Julie Kalsrap

In 2009 during my first flight to Vanuatu, a small island nation in the South Pacific just west of Fiji, I was filled with excitement. As the plane dipped below a layer of clouds, the intense green of the trees contrasted with the light blue of the water as the archipelago suddenly came into view. I had never been to the South Pacific, and while hopeful, I was anxious about beginning my fieldwork, and whether or not I would be welcome. Reflecting back on this today, I am aware of how different I was then as a person and researcher. On my eighth fieldtrip in February 2020 when my plane approached the islands, I saw the villages I now know well; the Port Vila coastline, dotted with familiar hotels and shops; and a towering cruise ship docked in the harbor. Rather than nervousness, I was full of joy and anticipation to reconnect with my friends and family, and to feel the embrace of home.

After completing month-long fieldtrips in 2009 and 2010, I returned to Vanuatu in 2012 with my husband, John, to conduct my dissertation fieldwork. I had collaborated with the Vanuatu Ministry of Health and the Vanuatu Cultural Centre to devise a study that would be useful to the government and public health officials, who were interested in qualitative data to contextualize decades of quantitative research documenting the ongoing problem of malnutrition in children under age five. I was broadly interested in food security and wanted to work with the Director of Public Health in order to produce research that would be beneficial. Across eight trips to Vanuatu, three of which John was able to accompany me for all or part of the time, I have been working to understand the different facets that shape feeding experience and contribute to childhood malnutrition, including behaviors and values surrounding breastfeeding and young child nutrition, the role of grandmothers in child feeding, the role of community feasts in promoting children's food security, urban gardening and urban land use change, and disaster response and the impact of Cyclone Pam on food access (see Wentworth 2016, 2017, 2019).

During my first two trips to Vanuatu, I rented a small room in the capital city, Port Vila. In 2012, after staying for two weeks with a friend employed by the Peace Corps, John and I set out to find a permanent residence for the year in Pango village, located twenty minutes by bus from Port Vila. We met Julie Kalsrap on our first trip to Pango. After looking at three houses for rent, we agreed to stay with her, her husband (also named John), and their two children, Kaltar and Leirick. Their third child, Wickliff, was born later that year. Moving in with the Kalsrap family was one of the most important decisions that John and I have ever made, as we now constitute a new family, our lives interwoven (see Figure 6.1). My primary goal in this chapter is to describe how this process of making a family, which began in 2012, has unfolded over the years for Julie and me.[1]

I felt strongly that in telling the story of creating our family, I needed to contextualize it within the discipline of anthropology's colonial history. Too many anthropologists have neglected or exploited what were intended to be reciprocal relationships. Julie was interested in this history and supportive of this need. We begin our story, therefore, with a brief discussion

Figure 6.1   A Family Photo in Front of Our Home. From the left, John, Julie, Wickliff, Chelsea, John. Second row, Kaltar and Leirick, 2015.

of anthropology's colonial legacy and the ways in which it impacts how anthropologists talk and write about fieldwork and families. Although a complete history of this topic is beyond this chapter's scope, our thinking about anthropological praxis, (de)colonization, kinship, and the creation of families draws on work from the 1960s to the present (e.g., Bowen, 1964; Briggs, 1986; Small, 1997, Gottlieb and Graham, 2012; West, 2016). We want to acknowledge this history and emphasize the critiques that have improved anthropological fieldwork today. In particular, we highlight the work of Indigenous scholars and build upon this scholarship by documenting our own process of creating our family (e.g., Smith, 2012; Trask, 1991; Kovach, 2010; Denzin, Lincoln, and Smith, 2008; Wilson and Yellow Bird, 2005). Finally, we reflect on this process in the context of decolonization and offer some thoughts about why this is important to anthropological praxis. We believe that this conversation is essential to training new scholars, improving our own work, promoting transparency in research, and revealing the ways in which reciprocity is embedded in our actions.

ANTHROPOLOGY AND COLONIALISM

Anthropology has a fraught relationship with colonialism. Essentialized visions of tropical villages and racist discourses of "primitive" people who live in tourist locales continue to dominate media images surrounding anthropological fieldwork, which further complicate anthropologists' work and the broader understanding of the discipline. The ideas of "discovering lost tribes" and "exploring exotic places" persist in the public imagination despite efforts to acknowledge the dangerous inaccuracy of these tropes and the damage of racist media discourse (Goldberg, 2018). A number of anthropologists have highlighted the persistent problems of this discourse that permeate demographic, medical, and development literature today (West, 2016; Jolly, 2007; Cummings, 2013; Abu-Lughod, 2008; Behar and Gordon, 1995). Many anthropologists who critique colonialism, however, also continue to benefit from colonial regimes.

"Armchair" anthropology, colonial expansion tied to anthropological practice, and pejorative discourses that indicate "ownership" of a host "family" have all been sharply, and rightly, criticized by Indigenous communities and scholars working to overcome inequalities in research praxis (Trask, 1991; Denzin, Lincoln, and Smith, 2008; Wilson and Yellow Bird, 2005). Important critiques of anthropology have come from Indigenous scholars, who question the discipline's abilities to offer more accurate and less damaging research. At the very least, Indigenous scholars writing about research praxis offer a more productive way forward for non-Indigenous anthropologists to engage with local communities (Smith, 2012; Awekotuku, 1999; Kovach, 2010; Chilisa, 2012).

One key realm of engagement is long-term fieldwork, a hallmark of anthropological research, which is still required for most doctoral students. Most academic and practicing anthropologists conduct long-term fieldwork precisely because of the benefits and knowledge that comes from working with a community for a long period of time, including the personal satisfaction provided by long-term relationships. Yet fieldwork is not always an easy or positive experience; it often involves danger and hardship (Samudra, 2015; Hess, 2011; Moreno, 1995). As Bacchiddu (2004:7) writes:

> Any anthropologist needs to be accepted by the community—and this implies not only downplaying differences but also engaging in a process of "imitation." The desire to feel part of the group and to succeed in creating ties—in order to conduct a successful research—has unexpected emotional consequences.

Despite anthropologists' ongoing efforts to establish rapport, fieldwork is often a lonely experience that creates a desire to forge lasting relationships, even friendships. But there are ways of doing this purposefully and critically that minimize negative consequences for communities (Briggs, 1986; Gottlieb, 1995). Thinking critically about the intentional cultivation of reciprocal relationships is one of the objectives of this volume, and certainly a primary aim of this chapter. Our goals are threefold. First, we explore the challenges associated with including research participants as coproducers of research and scholarly publications and how this exemplifies a form of reciprocity that is underrepresented in the anthropological literature. Second, we address the often taken-for-granted notion of fieldworker as family member by engaging research participants about what this means to them rather than simply accepting it as a given. Finally, we consider the challenges and limitations of coauthorship, especially as it is constrained by the rules and requirements of granting agencies and academic presses.

THE IDEA OF A HOST "FAMILY"

When anthropologists discuss their relationship with their host "families," these relationships often appear as unequal and reflect a model of fieldwork forged in the colonial era. After some graduate-level coursework, a woefully inexperienced graduate student travels to a remote location to conduct fieldwork. Following in the vein of Bronislaw Malinowski ([1922]1984), this novice anthropologist lives in a community for at least one (but ideally, two) years, learns the local language, and conducts participant observation with the goal of writing an ethnography of a group of people. When subsequent generations of anthropologists began to reflect on their ethnographic experiences in their published works (rather than limiting these to their fieldnotes and diaries), they revealed the challenges of debilitating illness, confronting their ethnocentrism, living with people with whom one does not share a language, and the triumphs of developing meaningful relationships (Bowen, 1964; Gottlieb and Graham, 2012). Indigenous scholars invested in bringing research findings back to their communities also brought the realities of these ethnographic encounters into the academic discussion, requiring anthropologists to face some uncomfortable truths.

As anthropologists expose the inherent difficulties of anthropological fieldwork—finding food, adequate shelter, and navigating a new cultural environment—they admit that local people often view them as unruly children capable of making costly errors within their host communities (Briggs, 1986). In many cases, a family or an individual emerges to help care for the anthropologist who bumbles along, making mistakes ranging from hilarious, to offensive, to dangerous (e.g., DeVita, 1990; Small, 1997; Knauft, 2009; Bowen, 1964). While anthropologists' accounts sometimes valorize host families or illustrate the fieldworkers' ineptitude, they rarely lead to necessary broader conversations about friendship, reciprocity, and the decolonization of research practice.

The process of creating families in fieldwork is unclear, even to anthropologists, whose job it is to understand the cultural dynamics of particular communities. Did this generous family know what they were taking on when they accepted the anthropologist into their home to live, or as their neighbor? Was this even the family's choice, or did a community authority assign members to care for this struggling outsider? How long did the family expect this relationship to last? What reciprocal expectations did the family have at the onset of the relationship? What happens when an anthropologist is unable to meet those expectations, or makes mistakes in the process? How do both sides negotiate reciprocity that is always imbalanced?

Simply because an anthropologist develops a relationship with a family does not necessarily mean that the family desires a permanent relationship with the anthropologist. Critical reflections on how such relationships should unfold and the problems they can cause remained largely unexplored until feminist and Indigenous scholars began highlighting them. Empowering participants in the research process is essential to participatory research practice. Participatory research (Shirk et al., 2012; Bibeau, 1997; Smucker et al., 2016; Kemmis and McTaggart, 2005), collaborative research (Lassiter, 2005b; Singer 1994), feminist research (Lather, 2001; Arvin, Tuck, and Morrill, 2013; Haraway, 1988), and Indigenous research (Deloria, 1969; Uperesa and Garriga-López, 2017; Tengan, 2002; Awekotuku, 2019) have all critiqued power and hierarchy in research over the past several decades (Flinn, Marshall, and Armstrong, 1998). This work is vital to understanding research dynamics and involving in meaningful ways research participants in scholarly work.

It would be beneficial if more anthropologists questioned the latent racism and colonialism that often shape the discourse of "family" in fieldwork. The ease with which anthropologists discuss host families as "their families," when they do not make such rapid associations with friends they encounter in their (Western) home countries, is problematic, and must be acknowledged and discussed—particularly in the training of new graduate students—if we want to make meaningful change. This is not to discount the family-like relationships that anthropologists regularly experience in their personal lives. Friends who help care for children or provide support during life challenges can in some cases become as or more significant than biologically related kin. Certainly, anthropologists have friends with whom they develop life-long bonds and whom they consider as "aunts," "uncles," "cousins," and "grand-parents." Those relationships, however, are maintained with expectations that are divorced from professional career advancement.

It is in this way that fieldwork-based relationships differ most significantly from the other long-term relationships that anthropologists develop in their personal lives. Research relationships are linked to financial security, promotion and tenure, and even notoriety for researchers, but communities or individuals within them rarely receive those same benefits. Furthermore, vastly different power and economic differentials distinguish the "family" relationships that anthropologists develop in the field from the ones they develop in their personal lives in their home countries. As such, fieldwork relationships require more nuanced understandings of reciprocal obligations (Brown, 2001). Nevertheless, anthropologists are also human, and it is unrealistic to expect them to suppress the emotional connections they develop to friends or "family" during their fieldwork, and to attempt to write from a purely objective perspective about them. Indeed, anthropologists become entangled in relationships in the field that are often deeply meaningful to all parties involved.

DEVELOPING RELATIONSHIPS AND MAKING FAMILY

When relationships and friendship bonds form, people often look for ways to label and acknowledge these ties. This is true with bonds formed during fieldwork. Earlier generations of anthropologists often directly identified themselves as belonging to a "family," using address terms, such as "mother" or "brother," without any discussion about the meaning behind them. When anthropologists enter particular communities, however, they must situate themselves within those communities in order to maintain broader structural relationships (Briggs, 1970). Developing kinship relationships serves to maintain existing social structures by lessening the disruptions that strangers and outsiders bring. As Kan (2001:3) explains:

> It is important to note that, from the Indian point of view, there is nothing particularly unusual about adopting an anthropologist, especially someone who has spent a great deal of time in the community and shows an understanding of cultural norms. Kinship, after all, has always been the central idiom of social relations in Native American societies.

The kinship relationships created to accommodate anthropologists, however, may be important in name, but less important in emotional connection. A host can be identified or recruited to provide accommodations for the visiting researcher, but that does not necessarily lead to the mutual emotional connection of a "family."

Alongside efforts to decolonize anthropology and improve research practices, many anthropologists have struggled with how to manage reciprocal relationships in the field. The reality is that many of these relationships are inherently political in ways that are often—at least, initially—unknown to the researcher. William and Margaret Rodman (1990), for example, describe their relationship with Bill's adoptive "father," Chief Mathias, after the crisis of Margaret's severe case of malaria while they were conducting fieldwork in Vanuatu. In reflecting on the nuances of this adoptive relationship, which Bill had originally misunderstood, he writes (Rodman and Rodman 1990:119):

> [Mathias] had adopted me; I interpreted that as having to do with kinship and amity, not politics. But Mathias understood something I did not: Ordinary sentiments of friendship and affection are inappropriate to extraordinary times. He is the chief of a territory—we were in his territory at the point at which Margy became ill. I assumed (incorrectly) that he would never try to impose his will on us. He assumed (incorrectly) that I would not challenge his decision in a time of crisis. Being in conflict with each other was a learning experience for us both.

Fieldwork relationships are more than kin-making practices and also reflect broader political relationships. Even if a researcher does not live with an elite family, his or her presence still intertwines with the adoptive family's reputation and status. Adopting a researcher can be a way for a family to exercise agency, exert power, and modify the existing social structure of the community. Kinship systems are powerful, and all actors in the system can access that power. Yet the ramifications of anthropologists' actions—such as failure to reciprocate appropriately—often reach beyond their immediate adoptive families and do not dissipate for community members as they often do for anthropologists when they leave the field. That is, while anthropologists can largely come and go as they please, the local people they work with cannot and thus must continue to live with the consequences of anthropologists' mistakes.

Despite the risks, developing and maintaining fieldwork "families" can be positive experiences for all parties involved. Acknowledging the creation of new family ties formed in fieldwork validates the work of relationships; it recognizes social status and justifies participation in community events. When anthropologists carefully examine these relationships, they co-create meaningful families in ways that shape how they proceed in their roles as researchers and family and community members. Juliana Flinn, for example, reflects on the first time that her "sister" used this kinship term to define their relationship. Flinn (1990:51) describes this as a turning point in her understanding of fieldwork families and, more generally, in her role as an anthropologist:

> First, I was able to take a very close look at the sort of role I wanted to play while living on the island. In this regard, I was made aware of how much my own values affected my behavior. Second, the abstract ideas I had read concerning kinship and Micronesian culture, instead of being an intellectual exercise, became very real and personal . . . [this] was the beginning of personal growth for me which led to the realization that I could do or say foolish things and still be valued and liked.

Honest reflections on the research experience are critical for anthropologists to read and consider in advance of conducting long-term fieldwork.

Acknowledging the process of developing relationships, Taylor (1991:244) writes, "The better the rapport and closer the relationships, the more likely people will feel used when the researcher starts to leave the scene or disappears altogether." Here, Taylor invites anthropologists to consider the impacts of their exit from the field. But he does not consider research participants' own preferences and desires for the future of the relationship. Ultimately, both parties need to agree to participate and establish some sort of reciprocal upkeep of the relationship in order for it to succeed. It is not always the case that both groups will want to maintain the relationship. But if anthropologists want to avoid colonial critiques, they need to acknowledge the power they hold in the physical act of leaving their fieldsite. In the spirit of efforts to decolonize anthropology, discussions of leaving the field must move beyond explaining that a researcher's involvement in the community is temporary and setting an exit date. Rather, researcher and community members should agree on how to practically manage the future and outcomes of the relationship.

Greater transparency and reflexivity also offer the opportunity for anthropologists to describe their own humanity in the context of fieldwork. At the most fundamental level, what anthropologists learn from these reflections is the embodied experience of the scholarly ideas of the late twentieth century, and what we teach in introductory anthropology courses: that kinship extends beyond bonds of consanguinity and affinity. Family relationships are characterized not just by biology, but also by shared emotions, behaviors, and relationships.

Yet recent scholarship, especially the work of Indigenous scholars (e.g., Smith, 2012; Denzin, Lincoln, and Smith, 2008; Kovach, 2010), urgently calls us to take this further, because rhetoric reinforces ideology, which reproduces structures of power and inequity (Hau'Ofa, 1994; West, 2017; Tengan, Ka'ili, and Fonoti, 2010). As researchers, we must think critically about how our presence in the field changes not just us as fieldworkers and human beings, but the communities where we work as well. Ethically, we are required to reflect on this impact, participate in difficult conversations, concede our failings, and build actions together that help reframe and reorganize a path forward that improves not only anthropological praxis, but also the communities with whom we live and work.

CREATING FAMILY IN VANUATU

The process of making families is deliberate, and it requires effort to navigate biological and created familial relationships. As humans, we have already developed a framework from our past that we can draw upon to help us navigate the process of making new relationships in fieldwork. One of our goals in this chapter is to describe our own process of creating family, not because it is perfect (it is not), but because we think it is essential that more field researchers carefully consider the ramifications of entering family relationships and the discourse surrounding those relationships. The construction of anthropological "families" is not so different from how we create other family relationships, yet the implications are profound and require context. To illustrate this idea, Julie and I worked together, writing and talking about our relationship, how it has evolved over time, and what is important about the process of making family. We wrote collaboratively over the course of two years the following descriptions of our relationship and how it developed. Below we describe in detail significant moments in the making of our own anthropological family. First, I describe my perspective on developing relationships with Julie and the Kalsrap family in Pango village, Vanuatu.

Then, Julie describes this relationship from her perspective, discussing the importance of familial reciprocity and expectations in cultural context.

We first began discussing the possibility of writing this chapter together over Facebook, after I had been in contact with this volume's co-editors about their goals for the book. Facebook is the primary way that Julie and I stay in touch during the time between my trips to Vanuatu. Immediately, I felt that my contribution about family should be cowritten, and I reached out to Julie to discuss it further. Julie was excited, but since this was her first involvement in writing for publication, she raised several concerns regarding her ability to contribute. While scholarly writing is important to my career, the benefits are less obvious for Julie. Because I wanted to write collaboratively, Julie contributed considerable time and effort beyond her daily routines to participate in this project. Joking about completing her "homework" assignments, Julie graciously participated in the process of producing knowledge that will be consumed primarily by an academic audience. However, copies of this volume will be stored in the Vanuatu National Library for all to access freely, and Julie will have copies to share in Pango.

Because Julie has been talking with me about my research and assisting with a range of logistical challenges during fieldwork over the past decade, she was familiar with the data collection process. While she has read my research publications and in fact has a copy of my dissertation at her home that anyone in Pango can read if interested, she had never learned about the academic writing process. Without access to a computer (Julie accesses Facebook Messenger on her mobile phone), it was difficult to have the conversations we needed to write the chapter together. Thus, when I was in Vanuatu in June and July 2018 for field research, we spent time discussing the project and writing the chapter. Julie wrote independently and then brought drafts to me with questions. I answered those questions and discussed with Julie the long process of peer-review and editing.

Revising the chapter proved significantly more difficult than composing the first draft. With a slow Internet connection in Vanuatu, downloading paper drafts was challenging, and we were unable to complete these tasks via Facebook Messenger while I was working in the United States. I worked with other researchers and friends in Vanuatu who had access to computers and printers, and who were willing to serve as intermediaries, to print and deliver drafts to Julie for review, but this was time consuming. Ultimately, we completed a bulk of the revisions during my fieldwork in February and March 2020. Publishing research and sharing it with community participants is challenging for researchers who work with communities that favor oral over written traditions, those who prefer that some knowledge not be transcribed into writing, or for researchers whose collaborators do not read or write. Julie and I both want to acknowledge that this collaboration is a privilege, as many research collaborators are not proficient in English or other common languages of publication or they lack the technology and networks to write collaboratively.

Julie is trilingual, fluent in Pango, her native Indigenous language, Bislama, Vanuatu's *lingua franca*, and English, the language she learned in school, which she attended through class 7. This level of schooling is very common in Vanuatu, as advancing to high school requires that families pay a substantial increase in fees that are cost prohibitive for most. Julie is not confident, however, in her ability to write in English, and chose to write her section of the chapter in Bislama. I then translated it into English, and Julie carefully edited it to ensure that my translation captured her intended meaning. Unfortunately, Lexington press restricts the number of "foreign" words in their publications. Although the volume's coeditors managed to negotiate up to 500 words, Julie's section was far longer than that. To meet the press's requirements, I cut some of the Bislama text, which is indicated with ellipses, and discussed this process with Julie. Julie's section that appears in English is an exact translation of what she wrote in Bislama, including the parts of the original Bislama text that I cut. Readers who are comparing the Bislama and English translation should be aware of this.

Julie and I value the Bislama language text both because it is Julie's actual voice, but also because it helps to share that voice with a ni-Vanuatu[2] audience (Keller and Kuautonga, 2008). Anthropological writings are often critiqued when they are not accessible to the communities with whom anthropologists work, which contributes to the broader neocolonial implications of some research. Furthermore, the primary publication venues that anthropologists choose (because they are required for tenure and promotion) are often behind paywalls that local collaborators can rarely penetrate. When published writings are available, they are usually written in English or another colonial language and very rarely in the first language of research participants from the global south.[3] It is difficult for anthropologists and other researchers to overcome the accusations of neocolonialism when they are limited by publishers in their efforts to do so. In the current volume, it is ironic that in a publication about reciprocity and the importance of meaningful engagement with research participants, contributors are limited in their ability to craft texts that best serve research and community partners. Nevertheless, Julie and I decided to contribute to this volume because we value our work with the volume's co-editors and other contributors and desire to make as much of this work available in Bislama as possible. We recognize that we would likely encounter the same challenge with other presses. We also appreciate the coeditors' encouragement to include this critical reflection on the writing and publishing process of our chapter and hope it will serve to promote dialogue on issues of reciprocity in the realm of publishing itself. We believe in transparency and access in publishing not only regarding work with Indigenous communities, but also for scholars who face barriers in career development and communities who participate in research, but often cannot access those publications (e.g., Amano, González-Varo, and Sutherland, 2016).

Discourses on Family from Chelsea

Like many nonbiological family relationships, Julie and I started out as friends. We spent hours together talking, cooking, and tending to children. During this time, I would regularly talk about my research. I feel strongly about making my work transparent and accessible, and Julie was interested from the beginning in learning about what I was doing. I also value input from others—particularly ni-Vanuatu—and Julie is a forthcoming advisor, not afraid to offer suggestions, corrections, and encouragement. Even as we were getting to know each other, Julie treated my work seriously, and pushed me to be a better fieldworker. In the first weeks that my husband, John, and I lived with Julie and her family, I told her that I needed to improve my Bislama language skills and asked her to avoid speaking English to me. I rarely heard a word of English from her after that. Furthermore, she regularly interrupted me when I was speaking to correct my grammar or pronunciation, a rare practice in ni-Vanuatu society, where people are extremely polite in overlooking speech errors. We would fall into fits of laughter as I failed to roll my r's or to make the right sounds with the placement of my tongue, particularly with the bits of Pango language that she taught me. Of course, my laughter made my speech worse. When reflecting on these memories, I can hear Julie's loud laugh, ending with a whooo-eee, ringing clearly in my mind. I know my Bislama is much better due to her efforts, and I am grateful that she was even more patient with my husband as he also learned Bislama.

Julie took an interest early on in my research on maternal and child health and nutrition. She has three children, the youngest of whom was born in the middle of my dissertation fieldwork. I would turn to her to talk through ideas, inquire about phrases or customs that came up during recent interviews, and ask for advice about exchanging gifts with interviewees. One afternoon, we sat in her living room next to a couch piled high with clean laundry. Julie was folding, while I was reading through questions I had written earlier for a survey I planned to administer at maternal and child health clinics. I was taking notes and editing with her help to ensure that I used appropriate language. She agreed to assist me with the pilot survey so that I could construct questions accurately, and I began to read the survey questions aloud, the way I planned to at health clinics.

On page two I read to her, "Who is the family member you turn to most often for medical advice for your children?" Julie responded, "you."

Assuming I had misunderstood, I said, "No, I want people to describe a family member here." Without missing a beat in folding toddler t-shirts, Julie said, "I know. You're the person in my family that I go to first when I have a question about my kids' health." A wave of emotion and honor washed over me, as I took in the implications of this short, but profound statement. I began to reflect upon and acknowledge the familial connection we were building together—the "adoption" that initially brought us together was developing deeper connections and responsibilities through our shared lives and values.

After that first reference Julie made to me as part of her family, we began to talk more about this. I wanted this to be clear between us so that we could meet each other's expectations. Part of this meant teaching me about family gift-giving, and the importance of partaking in ceremonies, to which we contributed as a family at weddings and other feasts. She advised John and me on how to give and receive gifts appropriately, how to participate in collective efforts to cook and serve food, and offered us space to demonstrate our commitment both to ni-Vanuatu culture and *kastom* and to our family (see Figure 6.2). This brought respect to both parties within the community; Julie and her family cared for us as new members of the community, and we responded in culturally appropriate ways, demonstrating what we had learned and how we were committed to contributing.

One weekend about seven months into my fieldwork, I went with a large group of people from Pango to the wedding celebration of a Pango woman who was marrying a man whose family lived a twenty-minute bus ride from Port Vila. Four or five different Pango bus drivers had volunteered to transport people into town for the final wedding feast. Each bus was brimming with riders and most of the adults had a child on their lap. Later that night when I returned home, I realized I had lost my mobile phone. I had used it on the bus for its flashlight feature but must have failed to put it back in my bag. I was disappointed, primarily because I had been storing contact names and phone numbers that I had failed to record elsewhere. Upset with myself for neglecting to create a backup list of contacts, I lamented to Julie about my lost phone, and my clumsiness in not keeping better track of it. She was surprised and recognized that the mobile phone—an inexpensive model I had purchased on my small budget—was far more important to me than it looked.

Two days later, I was writing fieldnotes in the evening, convinced that I would never see my phone again when I heard a knock on the door. When I answered it, I saw an unfamiliar teenage boy, timidly standing with his mother behind him. As he began to open his hand, his mother angrily pushed him forward, and he handed me my mobile phone, apologizing profusely for finding it on the bus and not immediately returning it. Thrilled at my luck, I thanked him and his mother, and she quickly pulled him away, swatting him on the arm and continuing to scold him loudly on the way back to the main

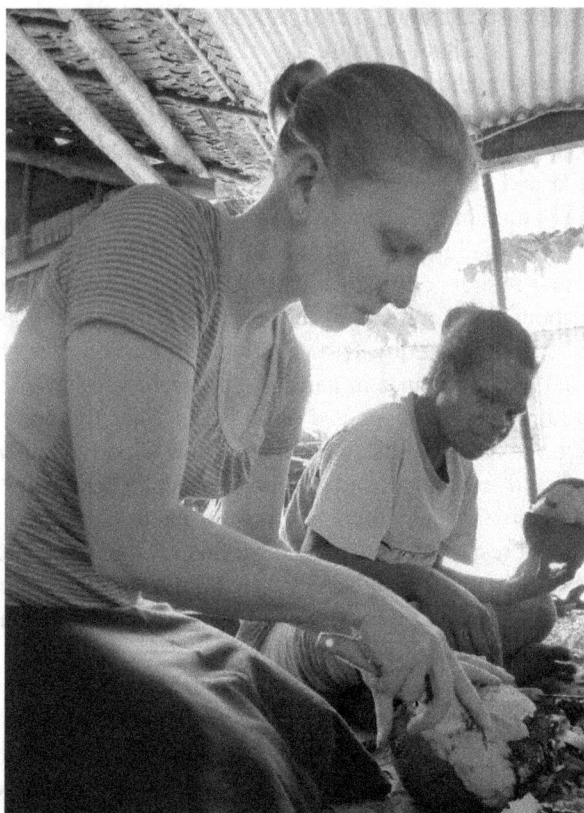

Figure 6.2   Julie, Ensuring That Chelsea is Properly Preparing Feast Food, 2012.
Photograph by John Fournier.

road. I hurried over to Julie to tell her my good fortune, and she nodded, unamused: "That never should have happened! I mentioned your phone to other women and knew that it would come back to you." Again, I saw the power and protection that come with being part of a family. The community acknowledged my membership in a family rather than as an outsider who would leave without any accountability or reciprocal relationships. How people treated me gradually shifted to mirror how they treated other community members.

For me, the most important part of joining a family was the love, hugs, and support that I received from everyone, particularly Julie's children. After a day of working in health clinics in Port Vila, I was still well down the worn footpath that crossed behind pigpens and backyard gardens on my walk home, when I heard tiny voices call out, "Chelsea, Chelsea!" Kaltar and Leirick would run and jump up into my arms, happy for me to be back home.

Other children began to follow their lead, and I regularly received seven or eight generous smiles and hugs. I do not have children of my own, and Julie has always been generous in sharing her children with me. I often work with mothers and children who are malnourished or sick, which can be emotionally challenging. When I began this work, I had no idea how important it would be to come home to my new family of happy, healthy children and to play with blocks, give snuggles, and read bedtime stories. Part of learning how to be a productive family member is reading expressive cues, being sensitive, and partaking in the emotional reciprocity imbedded in caring. In short, my family offered me the social support and joy that I needed.

As fieldwork comes to an end, anthropologists face the challenge of maintaining long-distance familial relationships. Julie and I are lucky to be able to use apps like Facebook Messenger to keep in touch between fieldtrips. Throughout my time in Vanuatu, John and I have helped in various ways, including paying school fees for Julie and her husband John's three children.[4] Among ni-Vanuatu family members, education is often a larger family discussion, and it is also common for ni-Vanuatu families to have relatives, such as aunts and uncles, who support the family with school fees. John and I view paying school fees not as a gift but as an investment in our family. Education supports children in their growth, empowers them to make their own choices, and creates future opportunities. It is a more parallel form of reciprocity. The support that I received from our ni-Vanuatu family directly impacted the success of my research—my ability to get both my Master's and Ph.D. degrees, my subsequent jobs and publications—all of which are related to my own educational goals and opportunities. That is, the educational opportunities that my husband and I provide for the children in our family feel appropriately matched by what Julie and her family provide us.

Storian long saed blong Family blong Julie

Fastaem we mi mitim Chelsea mo man blo hem, John, mi ting se bae tufala i olsem ol guest blo smol taem nomo. Mi bin ting se bae oli stap smol taem nomo afta bae tufala i kobak long kontri blo tufala mo afta foketem mifala.

Mi intres tumas lo Chelsea from taem mifala i storian wetem em lo kalja blo mifala em tu emi storian wetem mifala lo laef blo em (lukluk foto 6.3). So mifala i ekjanjem stori blo laef blo mifala. Emi wan samting we mi ting se mifala i tekem Chelsea mo John, we tufala i kam famli blo mifala. Afta tufala i giv han blong mifala bikwan blo karem ol pikinini blo mifala lo ospital mo tekem merisin blo olgeta from se emi hat blong tufala.

Emi kud tumas blo kat ol riserja olsem blo kam famli taem we i mekem olsem, from sam oli giv han plante, mo emi hat blong yumi . . . .Be sam lo ol riserja oli kam stap wetem wan famli lo Vanuatu, afta oli mekem wok blong olgeta, mo famli ia emi lukaotem kud olgeta. Be afta, oli kobak mo foketem famli ia we oli bin giv han long em. Emi no stret. So emi kud tumas blo yumi save kud ol riserja fastaem bifo yu tingting blong mekem emi famli blong yu. So taem we mifala i tekem Chelsea mo John i kam long famli blo mifala, mifala i wantem blong tufala i rispektem kalja blo mifala olsem. Tufala mas save olsem wanem mifala i sit daon blo kakae, o mifala i kukum kakae blo mifala, o taem we mifala i ko visitim ol olfalal man mo woman lo komuniti blong mifala. Oli mas save hao mifala i toktok lo ol narafala man, woman, mo pikinini.

(two paragraphs cut here)

(Beginning of paragraph cut here) . . . Chelsea emi stap wetem mifala klosap lo one yia. Taem we hemi stap long Pango, emi no haedem fasin blo em long mi. Emi helpem mi lo plante smol smol samting we mi nidim, mo taem emi stap helpem mi, mi mi trustem em from emi mekem evri samting lo hart blong em from mifala i famli. Mo tu mi mi mekem evri samting blong hart blong mi tu.

So naoia we Chelsea mo John tufala i famli blo mifala evrisamting we tufala i mekem tufala i talemaot lo mifala. Olsem tufala i bin move i ko lo narafala city, o John i bin kat niufala wok, o wan famli blo tufala i ded, bae tufala i letem mifala i save. Mo emi semak long mifala. Mifala i letem olketa i save evrisamting we ol famli blo mifala i mekem. Wanwan taem tufala i kolem mifala, be plante taem mifala i usem Facebook blong storian mo sarem laef taem we tufala i no stap. Chelsea emi kat mani blo ko mo kambak lo Vanuatu be emi no minim se emi bikwan bitim mi, from se mifala i kat kraon mo kastom storian we emi no kat so mitufala i kat semak value be emi tu difren samting.

Sipos wan ni-Vanuatu wantem kat wan riserja olsem famli blo hem, mekem sua se yufala i sitdaon tugeta mo storian kud blo save gud laef blong olgeta. Mo riserja i mas lanem kud kalja blo aelan, mo nasara blong yu. Emi importan we emi mas wantem lanem, yu no fosem em, from sipos no, bae emi ko mo nomo kambak.

Discourses on Family from Julie (English translation of the entire Bislama text)

When I first met Chelsea and her husband, John, I thought that they would be like guests or tourists that stay for a short time. I thought they would stay for a short while, and then go back to their country and forget us here. Or I thought we might be friends for a short time. But after they stayed with us for a while, I realized they were different than other guests. They were different in that they would come and sit and talk with us at length, and truly wanted to learn about our culture in Pango village.

Figure 6.3   Chelsea and Julie, Relaxing and Sharing Stories at the End of the Day, 2015.
Photograph by John Fournier.

I was very interested in Chelsea because when I would talk to her about our culture, she would then share information about her life. We exchanged stories of our lives (see Figure 6.3). This was the first thing that made us think that we should bring Chelsea and John into our family. They also loved our family and children, and we could see this in how they helped care for them by making sure they had medicine they needed and they took them to the doctor when they were sick.

It is very good to have a researcher with these values to enter your family because we help each other because of our family love. Also, they must really want to learn about our lifestyle in Vanuatu. However, some researchers come to Vanuatu, live with a family, do their work, and the ni-Vanuatu family cares for the researchers very well, but then the researchers leave and abandon their family relationships. This is not an appropriate practice. Therefore, it is very important for ni-Vanuatu to understand the behavior of the researchers before you think about bringing them into your family. That is why when we decided to bring Chelsea and John into our family, we made sure that they had respect for our culture. They needed to know how we eat together, cook together, and how we take care of the elders in our community. They also must know how to talk appropriately to men, women, and children.

I will give you some examples of how Chelsea and John demonstrate respect for our family. There was a time when Chelsea got very sick with a cold and flu. She was in pain, was throwing up, and had fever and cough. She felt really bad, and we knew that she missed her family at home, but they were all far away in the United States. Chelsea came to see us and told us how she was sick. We felt really bad for her because she felt so awful, so we made a big fire in our cookhouse, brought in a mattress and pillow and had Chelsea sleep there. Because Chelsea was coughing a lot, we made her hot water with lemon leaves, so that she could drink and ease her cough. Our mother, who Chelsea also calls "mom," came and massaged her body and sat with her for a long time. When she felt better, she went back to her house. We helped her the way that we help our family.

Additionally, Chelsea wanted to understand the customary marriage system in Pango. There was a woman who was married according to our customs. We must bring small gifts and presents including food from our gardens and food from the store. We put it all together and then we take it to the family of the woman who was getting married. Because Chelsea is our family, we told her about the day that we planned to present our gift to the woman's family. She went and bought some gifts and brought them to us. We put all of the gifts from our family together in one place and took it to present it to the family of the woman getting married. For a week we all came together at the house of the young woman's family. Chelsea and John took a lot of pictures of the wedding activities at home and at the church. Then Chelsea made some prints and put all the photos on a CD, and brought it to the father and mother of the woman who just got married. They were so happy to have these photos. And we were really happy to see that a researcher who had come into our family had done something special for a family that they did not know very well because they knew it was important to us.

Now Chelsea understands our culture very well. She speaks good Bislama and she is beginning to learn our language in Pango. Sometimes Chelsea makes a mistake in how she is speaking, and I must explain to her how that is wrong, and what she should do instead. Then she knows how to speak and act properly when she is working with others. After Chelsea had been with us for about one year, I knew that she did not change her behavior, or pretend for us. She helps us with some small things we need. When she shares ideas with us, I trust her because she is sharing her true heart and thoughts with us because we are family. And I, too, help Chelsea because we share family love.

Also, now that Chelsea and John are our family, everything that they do they must share with us. When they move to a new house or new city, or when John got a new job, or when someone in their family dies, they tell us so that we know about their life. And we do the same thing. We tell them about the things we are doing in our family. Sometimes they call us on the phone, but mostly we use Facebook to catch up, and continue to share our lives when they are not with us in Vanuatu. Chelsea has money to go to and from Vanuatu, but that does not mean that she is better or has more value than me, because we have land and cultural stories and understandings that she does not have, so together we each have the same value, we just have different things we bring together.

If a ni-Vanuatu family is thinking about having a researcher join their family, they need to make sure that they spend time talking together with the researcher to make sure you really understand the life and ways of the researcher. Additionally, the researcher must really understand the culture of your island, and the real meaning of your family's home culture. It is very important that they want to learn this; you cannot push them to do it, because if you force them, or they do not really understand, when they leave your home they will not come back or keep up the relationship.

REFLECTIONS ON RECIPROCITY IN THE
CONTEXT OF DECOLONIZATION

In analyzing reciprocity in fieldwork relationships, it is important to emphasize the role of reflexivity in the decolonization of research praxis. Central to the work of decolonization are efforts to involve research participants as cocreators of research and publications. Participatory approaches, however, only go so far; researchers still largely decide what to research, primarily due to preferences or requirements of the researcher's specialization or funding institutions. Researchers also often take a lead or sole role in writing up results, deciding what to include and where to publish findings. Many research participants are interested in collaborating and contributing to anthropologists' works, but the need for publications is often more relevant for professional anthropologists than it is for research participants. This is especially true for anthropologists working in communities across the global south. Anthropologists and research participants often have different goals and objectives. The motivation and benefits associated with engaging in a project for the research participants with whom anthropologists establish long-term relationships are often vastly different from those of the anthropologists themselves (Cummings, 2013).

Despite these shortcomings, participatory approaches, such as researcher/ community partnerships, can lead to new questions and have the potential to improve fieldwork relationships if anthropologists approach them with the goal of genuine reciprocity. What types of reciprocal relationships will anthropologists engage in, and for what duration? If anthropologists hope to call on research participants repeatedly in their fieldwork, how can they give back in recurring ways? What can anthropologists offer in such partnerships, and is what they offer valuable to research participants? Anthropologists need to move beyond small tokens of thanks for participation, which can have unintended consequences (Biruk, 2017), to larger ways of supporting those individuals who help anthropologists build their careers. Anthropologists must also critically examine how they value knowledge production, whose voice and knowledge are considered "expert" and why. These questions add significant time and work to the research process, including framing a project, evaluating grant applications and allocating budgets, and publishing results. In anthropological research, this can be a challenge as grants and research projects are often framed in the context of a year or a summer, despite the fact that these projects are often situated within much broader, long-term work.

In addressing questions about reframing their projects, anthropologists also need to consider the products they intend to produce. Frequently, researchers are vague about the goals and outcomes of their projects. Although research generates "knowledge," it does not automatically create positive outcomes for communities, nor do research projects typically come with funding for interventions based on research outcomes and recommendations. Particularly in applied contexts, it is easy for a research project to appear as part of a larger process of enacting tangible change. One goal of many anthropological projects is to provide "evidence" for interventions and public policy that aim to be "evidence-based." Transforming research into policy or programmatic interventions, however, is often beyond the scope of anthropological research. Therefore, it is imperative that anthropologists clearly communicate this at the beginning of their projects to avoid disappointing or misleading members of the communities in which they work. As anthropologists are often in a position of power within a community (at the very least, they have research funding), it is easy to see how local people might view them as wielding more authority to enact change than they actually possess. Anthropologists cannot require governments or policy makers, for example, to implement the changes that they recommend. But to many outsiders unfamiliar with the research process, this is not always evident.

In part because of the changing nature of research funding and university employment, ethnography is rarely conducted for the sole purpose of documenting and describing a culture group, as it often was in the past (Zimmer-Tamakoshi, 2018). "Practical" applications and contributions to broader scientific knowledge are critical in shaping the structure of ethnographic research today. With this shift, it is now common for anthropologists to live in communities in which research participants are no longer members of a single extended family. Many anthropologists now spend the bulk of their time working with government ministries, local NGOs, community groups, and families from different neighborhoods and cities (e.g., Hardin and

Kwauk, 2019; Pfeiffer and Chapman, 2010; Janes and Corbett, 2009). This does not, however, diminish the role that host families play in the research process. These relationships are often essential to networking, language learning, and providing ethnographic insights. In some cases, anthropologists train indigenous partners in fieldwork methods and enlist help with data collection, transcription, and analysis. Even if the community in which an anthropologist lives is not part of the research itself, relationships form, expectations develop, and the challenges of reciprocity ensue.

Despite anthropologists' best efforts to be inclusive, respectful, and collaborative, they often fall short of the work needed to decolonize the discipline. Indigenous anthropologists continue to advocate for more inclusive, collaborative research practices, and for research to provide tangible benefits to their communities. Bentz (1997:130) writes: "Increasingly, Native Americans everywhere will require that anthropological research in their communities serve humanity, as it should have all along, and will no longer allow humanity to serve science, as it often has in the past." This is a challenge to anthropologists everywhere to think creatively and, more importantly, collaboratively, with community members as they (re)consider the role of reciprocity moving forward. Collaborative writing serves as one important way of highlighting research participants' voices, and reflexive conversations about family can help anthropologists manage relationships in and beyond fieldwork. By working collaboratively with community members in both research and writing, anthropologists can link discussions of reciprocity with wider efforts to decolonize research praxis and the discipline, more broadly.

CONVERSATIONS ABOUT FAMILY: A WAY FORWARD

Anthropologists know that biology alone does not make families. They also know that family relationships are complicated. While biological ties can feel strong and supportive, they do not necessarily create deep emotional bonds; indeed, they can even be toxic or abusive. Found and created family ties can be essential to long-term happiness and well-being, but they can also fade over time as different sets of relationships take more or less prominence in individuals' lives. The making of families is not unique to fieldwork practice; all people make choices about how to engage with family, who is included in the group, and how to define and redefine interactions and obligations within family networks. People move between and among different families, including those based on biology and marriage and those based on emotional or financial support. All of these relationships are both dynamic and deeply meaningful to human experience.

Family relationships, however they are formed, also require considerable work. Anthropologists' conversations about their fieldwork families can sometimes sound self-indulgent, but they are essential to the engaged practice of fieldwork, the production of knowledge, and the decolonization of research praxis. Conversations are important to have, I suggest, regardless of whether or not anthropologists enter into "family" relationships in the field. Engaging in reflexive dialogue strengthens relationships. Relationships forged through anthropological fieldwork require no less work than those of biological or chosen families. In fact, the former require more purposeful discussion in an effort to ensure that relationships develop in ways that benefit all parties involved. Reflecting on fieldwork-based relationships is important to the practice of decolonizing research in a meaningful way (Calderon, 2016).

To truly cultivate an anthropological "family" requires an ongoing commitment and open understanding and agreement by *both* parties, anthropologist and research participants. Acknowledging the distinctions between members, the strengths and weaknesses that each party brings to the relationship, and how to improve communication and collaboration are essential to the success of these relationships. In so doing, anthropologists can transition decolonization from a metaphor to a source of real change (Tuck and Yang, 2012). Through working on this project, Julie and I argue that reframing the discourses involved in making anthropological "families"—so that all parties are empowered—is critical to the decolonization of fieldwork. It is not enough for academics to have these conversations among themselves; research participants and fieldwork partners must participate equally in meaning-making processes and critiques.

Anthropologists need to have conversations about the nature of reciprocity and the decolonization of fieldwork with their graduate students and with other scholars, so that discourses of anthropological "families" can acknowledge and respond to the discipline's colonial legacy. Julie and I are convinced that discussing this openly is the only way to work toward creating relationships that empower all parties and support the advancement of the discipline of anthropology.

Ultimately, no amount of discussion can erase either the colonial legacy or the ongoing power disparities inherent in anthropological research. Nevertheless, it is critical to have these conversations, to integrate more reflexivity into anthropological research, and to think critically about the creation of fieldwork "families" and the meaning of reciprocity in ways that inspire actionable change. Anthropologists can never fully escape the legacy of colonialism out of which our discipline was born. That does not preclude us, however, from actively engaging and working to create a better future for the people with whom we work—friends, "family," and research participants—and for the discipline as a whole.

NOTES

1. Acknowledgments: Many thanks to Sarah James and Alie Harris for helping us share drafts over long distances. Profound thanks to the co-editors of this volume for being supportive of our long process and encouraging of our critiques. Julie would like to thank John Kalsrap, Issac and Mercy Thomas, Leiser Sogari, Martha Kalsrap, and Dainah Simeon. Chelsea would like to thank John Fournier, the ni-Vanuatu research participants who shaped her research and career, and her whole Vanuatu family and community for their love, kindness and continued support.

2. Ni-Vanuatu is the term, chosen at independence, that refers to Indigenous people from Vanuatu. Ni-Vanuatu is both singular and plural.

3. Recent exceptions include the publication of abstracts in Tok Pigin in the journal *American Ethnologist* (Handman 2017).

4. We have contributed to both public and private school fees. The experience and quality of private schooling in Vanuatu is substantially different from public school (which still requires families to pay annual fees per child, and cover supplies and required uniforms).

Afterword

Concluding Thoughts on Fieldwork and Friendwork

Alma Gottlieb

The sacrosanct gift of invitation into others' lives brings with it the equally sacrosanct obligation to consider appropriate ways to repay that gift. In that sense, Marcel Mauss not only lies at the heart of every one of these chapters—in one way or another, his early masterpiece, *The Gift* (2016[1925]), lies at the very heart of the ethnographic endeavor.

But that obligation is, itself, multistranded. As Mauss recognized, reciprocity may be immediate or delayed; equal or unequal; secular or underpinned by spiritual foundations; financial or social; and optional or legally binding. Accordingly, in essays that are as lyrically written as they are refreshingly (sometimes, brutally) frank, the uniquely riveting chapters of this collection remind us that reciprocity takes many forms. Moreover, in some cases, "gift" per se may not be the most accurate trope for imagining the complex relations that undergird the ethnographic project (as one contributor, Carolyn Rouse, explicitly outlines). Attentive ethnographers forge locally appropriate models of reciprocity in the ethnographic cauldron in which they live and work.

In her chapter in this volume, Michelle Johnson confides that in a village in Guinea-Bissau, a holy man's prognosticatory dream about her eventual arrival "raised questions . . . [she] still struggle[s] to answer today." That is a productive place from which to begin this final discussion precisely because questions about how we go about doing the intimate work we do as ethnographers go to the heart of our discipline and, therefore, demand continually to be addressed. If extended fieldwork distinguishes us from our sister social sciences, what obligations does that fieldwork entail at the human level—both for us, and for our interlocutors? It is critical to remember, as Josh Fisher writes in these pages, that "we are not 'experts' because of our position as anthropologists; rather, we owe our expertise to the bundles of relations that make, and have made, our knowledge possible." In economistic terms, what are the costs and benefits of the debt that is inevitably created for all ethnographers from any ethnographic engagement?

We now have a robust corpus of fieldwork memoirs that chronicle the actual experiences of "being there," as one collection of short memoirs is titled (Konner and Davis, 2011). These experiences range from friendship (Grindal and Salamone, 2006) to danger (Howell, 1990; Ice, Dufour, and Stevens, 2015), including rape (Moreno, 1995), and everything in-between. Individual works sensitively think through the specificities of fieldwork challenges, including classic memoirs (sometimes semi-fictionalized and/ or written pseudonymously) by Behar (1995), Bowen [Bohannan] (1964), Cesara [Poewe] (1982), and Stoller and Olkes (1987), and many others since then. Thankfully, we have come a long way from the day back in 1985 when a dean asked me during an interview for a tenure-track job to list the courses I might like to teach, and my first thought was, *A course in field methods*— precisely because no such course had been offered during my own graduate school training, and I sorely missed its absence while conducting my challenging doctoral research in rain-forest villages of West Africa (cf. Gottlieb and Graham, 1994).

Once I accepted that teaching position, creating such a course became one of my first commitments. I taught versions of the class over a dozen times— but the more I taught it, the more I concluded that, for students, taking such a seminar was just the beginning. Far from walking away from the classroom with everything they needed to know about "how to do fieldwork," students, I determined, should walk away with a sense that they could never learn "how to do fieldwork"—at least, not in any formulaic way. Rather, they could—and should—learn how to think critically about the challenges posed continually by such research. And, after an intense semester's worth of readings in fieldworking anthropologists' experiences and reflections, students would emerge with a repertoire of headnotes that, in the best of circumstances, could intelligently inform the decisions they would have to make, often at the spur of the moment, concerning the future dilemmas that they would inevitably face in their own fieldwork—dilemmas that might well encompass ethical, emotional, political, financial, legal, and other challenges.

In fact, every time I taught the course, I rebalanced the ratio of time I spent on pragmatic vs. ethical challenges—always moving in the direction of ethics. After several years of teaching the course, ethics entirely eclipsed pragmatics as the focus—precisely because ethical issues lie so centrally at the heart of the work we do as ethnographers. As such, ethical issues may sometimes feel overwhelming, because of competing claims from different people and institutions within a single "fieldwork community." That "inconvenient truth" (as Al Gore might put it) brings us to this collection.

Despite the now rich corpus of fieldwork memoirs chronicling individual experiences of ethnographic encounters, still missing from much of this corpus is a systematic discussion of the ethical responsibility of the engaged ethnographer. How does the mandate for reciprocity actually play out—both during the ethnographic encounter (whether the fieldsite is distant or nearby), and after we leave? The complexities of our multiple relations with women and men, children and adults, each inhabiting their own social spaces and subjectivities, may make for a troubling fieldwork experience. In this volume, Josh Fisher hints at one scenario embedded in this critical question, in the title of his chapter: What happens when the ethnographer risks becoming perceived as "brother [or sister] to a scorpion"?

Regardless of the complexities of specific scenarios, at base, the lesson of ethical challenges is simple: as ethnographers, we must commit to remaining engaged. As Fisher also writes, "And becoming an anthropologist is a debt that can never, really, be dispatched. It is a life's work." The scholars whose thoughts are collected in this important volume have all shared their candid and moving reflections on the many contours that such debts—and their partial repayments—may take.

The authors of these chapters have each had long engagements with their host communities: if I've got my math right, ten years for Chelsea Wentworth, thirteen years for Josh Fisher, fourteen years for Caroline Rouse, twenty-four years for Michelle Johnson, twenty-nine years for Ned Searles, and a whopping fifty-three years for Anya Royce. And counting. That's a grand total of 143 years, collectively. As such, these scholars represent the opposite of the dreaded, commando-raid style of fieldwork that sometimes gives anthropology a bad name and earns us the dreaded accusation of neocolonialist. You know the now-notorious model: go somewhere exotic for a year, write a dissertation, build a lucrative career based on that thesis, and never return to the community.[1] Sadly, few anthropologists manage to keep up mutually productive relationships with the members of their host communities across multiple generations. In that sense, the authors of the chapters in this volume represent the ideal scenario. Their decades-long commitments allow them to remain, as Royce put it, "engaged in the hermeneutics of learning . . . and once you admit the possibility of dialogue, you open the door to the unknown and the unpredictable."

Splashing through the choppy waters of "the unknown and the unpredictable," the stories we have read across these pages all chronicle multisensory experiences. Their ethnographers have not just scooped up data like a vacuum cleaner, put them in a theory processor, and pressed *Blend* to produce theoretically informed analyses that speak to disciplinary models. Rather, they have tried, as Royce has put it here, to "plant your feet in the earth of the path, listen to the songs of the prayer-leader, feel the heat, smell the wild, eat the tamales offered pilgrims along the way, arrive at the foot of the mountain."

Even so, immersing oneself in the multimodal experiences of another place is just the beginning. The more immersed we become, the more our hosts expect of us. And, rightly so. Why should they accept an uninvited stranger into their communities and homes without expecting appropriate compensation? But the forms that such compensation may—and should—take can diverge dramatically even at the material level. The authors of these essays have recounted forms of compensation ranging from bars of soap or packs of cigarettes to vehicles and large amounts of cash. But even this wide variety does not encompass the options. At the more immaterial level, our authors' efforts at compensation have ranged from names to quotidian kinship obligations to ongoing support of education. Let us begin with the material plane.

During his first stay with Inuit communities, Ned Searles wished he could have bought plenty of locally valued commodities for his hosts. However, his meager graduate student budget proved hopelessly insufficient. Ruminating with rare honesty about the constraints of his graduate student-era economic situation, Ned relates that, in the end, he emerged with substantial credit card debt, so as to be able to contribute to community well-being. Ned found a valuable ethnographic lesson in that financial commitment. He writes: "Working without enough money to pay for food, lodging, and interviews provided me an opportunity to learn and follow the Inuit rules of reciprocity in order to survive."

At the same time, if capitalism emphasizes gifts of monetary value, nevertheless, as Searles points out, gifts of monetary value may not be wholeheartedly welcomed in communities that prize social ties more than individual accumulation. In Nicaragua, as Josh Fisher points out, individuals who indulge in excesses of capitalist accumulation are unflatteringly dubbed "scorpions."

As Fisher elucidates, for Nicaraguans, humans-as-scorpions represent a powerful anti-model for prized behavior. In explaining his interest in totemism, Lévi-Strauss (1963:89) once wrote, animals are "good to think [with]" (cf. Tambiah, 1969). Keeping Lévi-Strauss's homily in mind in analyzing Beng myths about dogs, I once described animals as

creatures that can resonate symbolically . . . [insofar as they present] a ready sense of "Other" that humans have often taken as a contrast or counterpart to themselves. Put another way, we have used animals to present to ourselves the negative traits of our own humanity. (Gottlieb 1986:485)

Paying attention to the morality tales contained in animal narratives such as the "selfish scorpion" can inspire us to think creatively about how best to forge locally appropriate means for going some way to repay our hosts for the invaluable gift of their welcome, their multiple forms of knowledge and expertise, and even our adoption into their families.

How do we appropriately compensate such host communities, while avoiding creating social rifts among community members who are jealous over unequal gifts? Searles wisely opted for the extended loan of a snowmobile, as an appropriate way to help a family as a social unit—rather than gifting smaller objects to individuals, which might have pitted them against each other. Only when we discern such ethnographically critical values, and study local gifting practices as a basis for operationalizing those values, can we contribute as respected, and respectful, participants in our host communities—rather than, say, as resented "scorpions."

In her chapter here, Michelle Johnson acknowledges the importance of economically valuable gifts, but she also points out that "priceless" gifts lacking monetary value—including the gift of a name—can provide different forms of mutual satisfaction. As anthropologists, we know how symbolically potent names are in virtually all social settings.[2] In Johnson's case, a little girl named after her ended up feeling empowered not only to pursue but even excel in a local Qur'anic education normally only available to boys. In this case, the unplanned gift of a name transformed a young girl's otherwise gendered fate. "Money often gets lost or stolen," Michelle writes movingly, "mud bricks collapse and paint fades over time, but names outlast them all: transcending distance and even death, they prevent people from forgetting."

My husband, Philip Graham, and I learned a related lesson when our son Nathaniel was renamed "N'zri Denju" in a Beng village. This was no ordinary "day name," as my husband and I had been assigned (Kouadio/Tuesday for Philip, Amwe/Sunday for me). Rather, Nathaniel received the name of a revered matriclan ancestor ("Grandfather Denju"), whose reincarnation our then-six-year-old son had suddenly become. That gift—bestowed on, rather than by, our family—had permanent repercussions for our childrearing practices, as the elder who conferred the name outlined the parenting requirements for a child-who-was-also-an-ancestor.[3] Our son, now an adult, relates that it also affected his own sense of self for many years into his childhood. And just months before this book went to press, some twenty-seven years after that naming ritual, a reverse naming practice entered our lives, as our informally adopted Beng son (now, a professional living in Abidjan) emailed me that his pregnant wife was requesting permission to name the daughter still in her womb, Alma. Of course, such honors come with obligations, and the cycle of reciprocity that enmeshed us across these decades has taken a new path as I contemplate the gifts to best honor this future namesake across the ocean.

Two-way naming practices such as these constitute rich ground for ethnographic inquiry. What are the sociological implications for anthropologists when they (or their accompanying family members) receive local names in host communities? Or, when they decide to name their own children using names from their former host communities, as Johnson and Searles have also done? Or, reciprocally, when members of host communities name their own children for visiting anthropologists? In all those scenarios, what obligations, gifts, entanglements, and misunderstandings have flowed in both directions from these cross-cultural naming rituals? The ethical, financial, legal, and emotional implications of this multiply-complicated social praxis beg for further discussion.

In this collection, Chelsea Wentworth tackles related questions with admirable honesty in the context of her own fieldwork in Vanuatu. In her chapter, Wentworth revisits a venerable topic in cultural anthropology, that of "fictive kinship."[4] Rather than taking at face value the common practice of fieldworkers being "adopted" into host families in their research venues, Wentworth looks critically at what host families expect of such "adoptions."[5] Not only does she chronicle the continuing responsibilities she faces toward her adoptive family in Vanuatu, but she has invited her host/adoptive sister, Julie Kalsrap, to author a section of her chapter addressing this important question from her own perspective.

To date, few anthropologists have embraced this sort of reciprocal writing strategy. Yet, as Wentworth's chapter exemplifies, if the circumstances are workable and the relevant parties agreeable, coauthorship may prove a mutually rewarding option for scholars seeking creative means to collaborate with fieldwork consultants on an equal basis. And, as Wentworth also points out, such collaborations should also make for far more ethical engagements. A recent book co-authored by a Spanish duo exemplifies just such a refreshing collaboration. Anthropologist, Paloma Gay y Blasco, has partnered with her long-time Roma fieldwork consultant-turned-friend, Liria Hernández, to coauthor a full-length, joint ethnographic memoir about their decades-long relationship; that remarkable book may well serve as a model for future ethnographic writings (Gay y Blasco and Hernández, 2020).

Yet, commendable as they are in theory, such coauthorships may not prove practical in all ethnographic situations. A given anthropologist and field collaborator may lack the technical means to remain in the continued close contact that coauthorship requires. (Wentworth mentions this as a troublesome hurdle for her and her Vanuatu coauthor, Julie Kalsrap, although the pair resolutely managed to find effective means to communicate and collaborate across great distances.) An otherwise engaged fieldwork collaborator may lack any interest in coauthorship. Drastic disparities in formal educational backgrounds may make coauthorship awkward. The latter challenge finds discussion elsewhere in this volume.

Several contributors to this collection seek means to level out the world's unequal access to resources via education. Given that (as of 2014), only 43 percent of the planet's young people had completed high school (UNESCO n.d.), the common claims we see in the mass media that we now live in a "hyper-connected, global village" are, as Johnson reminds us in her chapter, as yet entirely un-met for much of the human population, especially those in the global south. Providing means to pursue education, especially at higher levels—whether locally or abroad—is one richly rewarding strategy that visiting anthropologists might provide in some ethnographic settings. As Johnson relates in her chapter, she and her anthropologist husband supported an education in Algeria for a young Guinean man that eventually yielded the student a lucrative government position back in Guinea-Bissau. Similarly, Wentworth relates that she has paid local school fees for the three young children of her Vanuatu collaborator. Such laudable efforts transform individual lives.

In this collection, Carolyn Rouse chronicles an extraordinary endeavor at another level. With brutal honesty, Rouse records the many political, economic, logistic, legal, and emotional challenges she has confronted as she worked to create a private high school in Ghana. Those struggles ranged from sexism and racism that unexpectedly faced Rouse in Ghana, to charges of neocolonialism that she encountered in engaging with scholarly colleagues in the United States. Caught between a veritable Scylla and Charybdis of transcontinental critiques, Rouse persevered, motivated by a commitment to do what she could to help offset what she terms the "existential debt" created by the Euro-colonial invasion of Africa. Rouse's ability to envision, raise funds for, populate, administer, and sustain a high school in Accra while permanently based in New Jersey was, doubtless, the result of multiple factors, including personal grit and resilience, for starters, combined with the powerful resources of her home institution of Princeton University.

In contemplating how to forge the widest possible impact in our fieldwork communities, few anthropologists likely have such resources on which to draw. Nevertheless, an inability to create systematic opportunities can gnaw on our conscience. Key to envisioning realistic projects is one's stage in the life cycle. It is hard to imagine how an untenured assistant professor might have implemented the sort of project that Rouse undertook. Likewise, it would have been more challenging to build a school by a scholar based on a campus with far fewer economic resources than those of Princeton. Being realistic about what we can do at different stages in our career—as well as different stages in the lives of our ethnographic interlocutors, and different moments in the political histories of our fieldsites—is critical to crafting projects that are not only admirable but also viable.

Early in my own fieldwork in Côte d'Ivoire, my husband and I committed to investing in community projects in the Beng villages that had hosted us. Philip and I eventually created a non-governmental organization dedicated to this goal, but it took some 35 years for the circumstances to become both politically feasible and pragmatically workable. In the meanwhile, we privately funded development projects in two Beng villages, and we supported the eldest son of our third village host in Bengland, bringing him to the United States to continue his college studies. Bertin's parents agreed to the plan only after Philip and I consented to serve as Bertin's American parents.[6] In the end, Bertin stayed in the country for 19 years—completing a BA in political science at our university, then an MA in African studies there, then a PhD in international relations at another university. Playing the role of proud mother, I flew to Florida for Bertin's PhD graduation, then watched with more maternal pride as he started a tenure-track position teaching at a small college in Pennsylvania. Soon afterward, Bertin drove to Illinois to attend the high school graduation of our daughter—his quasi-adopted sister. Now, with Bertin in Côte d'Ivoire, our trans-Atlantic relationship continues over Zoom (see Figure A.1).

These long-term bonds of reciprocity were immensely satisfying at the individual level for all of us. But behind this gifting of funds into one individual

Figure Afterword.1   A Zoom Call with Our Extended, Trans-Atlantic Family, 2020. Top row (left to right): Nathaniel Graham, Dean Graham, Emily Graham, Alma Gottlieb, Philip Graham. Bottom row (left to right): Andrew Samuels, Hannah Gottlieb-Graham, Alma Princesse Aya Kouadio, Monique Amoin Coulibaly, Bertin Kouakou Kouadio, Brandon Alvinn Kouassi Kouadio.

lay a longer-term, community-level plan. Eventually, we hoped, Bertin would return to Côte d'Ivoire, where he could parlay his prestigious U.S. education into systematic help for his natal community. The plan became delayed for many years due to alternating political unrest and out-and-out civil war in Côte d'Ivoire. Likewise, many years have passed since Philip and I last lived in Bengland. During the nation's difficult years, we struggled to stay in touch with, and maintain our obligations to, our village families, friends, and hosts. Once his home country became relatively stable, Bertin gave up his U.S. professorship and moved back to Abidjan, where he has taught at local universities and has held a high-level position in the government. When Bertin returned to his home country, Philip and I were finally able to legally establish the Beng Community Fund (BCF), thereby entering us into a new chapter in our engagement with the Beng.[7] The BCF now enacts village development projects organized and administered by Bertin, and the story of our lifelong relationship with the Beng continues. Perhaps our "delayed reciprocity" is a variation of those intergenerational marital systems of family and clan alliances analyzed long ago by Lévi-Strauss (1969).

If it feels hard enough to maintain support—emotional, financial, and otherwise—for a single host community over the course of our lifetime, how can we possibly maintain such support in multiple communities when we do multisited research? In fact, multisited research projects are now becoming more the norm than the exception for many anthropologists (e.g., Balasescu, 2007; Coleman, 2006; Falzon, 2016; Hannerz, 2003; Marcus, 1998; Wulff, 2002). The question of how to uphold ethically engaged relations in more than one community therefore deserves extended consideration. My own current research faces this challenge. For the past ten years, I have been working with Cape Verdeans in diasporic sites around the world. The project began in Lisbon, expanded to New England (where I am now based), and has encompassed short research trips to Paris and several Cape Verde islands, as well as interviews (some online) with Cape Verdeans in places as far-flung as Rotterdam and Arizona (Gottlieb, 2012a). The challenges of maintaining meaningful forms of reciprocity when conducting fieldwork in such multiple and distant sites constitute a pressing contemporary issue that the authors of these pages do not address at length. Perhaps that will be the focus for a sequel.

For now, I expect that the insightful chapters of this collection will stay with you as you contemplate the next phase of your own fieldwork commitments. Whether you are currently planning a new fieldwork project or are already immersed in one or more long-term fieldwork engagements, the stories you have read in these pages should provide ample thoughts, perhaps even models, for forging your own continuing bases for reciprocity with those in your host communities.

Nowadays, most cultural anthropologists acknowledge that ethnographic research by definition revolves around not just social relations among residents of a "field community" but also social relations that enmesh the "observing" anthropologist. And, as virtually all philosophers would assert, human relations by definition involve ethical challenges. Braiding together the hermeneutic foundations of ethnography with the ethical foundations of hermeneutics leads us to a particular vision of the ethnographic project. That vision itself suggests the discipline of anthropology as one rooted in an ethical imperative stemming from both the knowledge gained from the ethnographic endeavor, and the human relations that "produced" that knowledge.

With these insights in mind, I consider it appropriate to leave the last word to Jane Addams, the American political reformer whose feminist and other social activism was firmly based in critical reflection of the society in which she lived. I imagine the deeply thoughtful contributors to this volume would heartily endorse Adams's claim of long ago: "Action indeed is the sole medium of expression for ethics" (1902:273).

NOTES

1. For a different perspective on the decision to end conducting research in one fieldsite and move to another, cf. Gottlieb (2012b).

2. For two classic studies, see Geertz and Geertz (1964) and Lévi-Strauss (1966); for later collections of essays on the subject, see Tonkin (1984), vom Bruck and Bodenhorn (2006), and, more recently, Hough (2016).

3. We chronicle this component of our fieldwork experience in *Braided Worlds* (Gottlieb and Graham 2012).

4. The classic, early case for all kinship systems being "fictive"—in the sense of being culturally constructed, rather than biologically given—was made by Schneider (1980[1968]) and developed by his student, Wagner (2016). A few more recent discussions of different components of the "all-kinship-is-fictive" model include Anderson (2012), Kim (2009), Levine (2008), McKinnon and Franklin (2000), Schneider (1997) and Weston (1997).

5. For a recent, brief but provocative look at unexpected "host family" experiences of an American anthropologist in Jordan, see Patterson (2012).

6. This episode finds fuller discussion in Gottlieb and Graham (2012).

7. For more about the BCF, see its webpage: http://almagottlieb.com/research-publications/bcf/; and its Facebook page: https://www.facebook.com/bengcommunityfund/

Works Cited

Abu-Lughod, Lila. 1990. "Can There Be a Feminist Ethnography?" *Women and Performance: A Journal of Feminist Theory* 9:1–24.

———. 2008 [1991]. "Writing Against Culture." In *The Cultural Geography Reader*, edited by Timothy S. Oakes and Patricia L. Price, pp. 50–9. New York: Routledge.

———. 2013. *Do Muslim Women Need Saving?* Cambridge: Harvard University Press.

Addams, Jane. 1902. *Democracy and Social Ethics*. New York: Macmillan.

Alvarez, Sonia. 2009. "Beyond NGO-ization? Reflections from Latin America." *Development* 52(2):175–84.

Amano, Tatsuya, Juan P. González-Varo and William J. Sutherland. 2016. "Languages are Still a Major Barrier to Global Science." *PLOS Biology* 14(12):e2000933. doi:10.1371/journal.pbio.2000933.

Anderson, Ryan. 2012. "Kinship: Real, Imagined, Past & Present," *Anthropologies: Collaborative Online Project* 9 (special issue: Kinship in the 21st Century). Online: http://www.anthropologiesproject.org/2012/04/kinship-real-imagined-past-present.html.

Arvin, Maile, Eve Tuck and Angie Morrill. 2013. "Decolonizing Feminism: Challenging Connections between Settler Colonialism and Heteropatriarchy." *Feminist Formations* 25(1):8–34.

Ashraf, Quamrul and Oded Galor. 2013. "Genetic Diversity and the Origins of Cultural Fragmentation." *American Economic Review: Papers and Proceedings* 103(3):528–33.

Auyero, Javier and Débora Alejandra Swistun. 2009. *Flammable: Environmental Suffering in an Argentine Shantytown*. New York: Oxford University Press.

Awekotuku, Nhahuia Te. 1999. "Maori Women and Research: Researching Ourselves." Maori and Psychology Research Unit, Hamilton.

———. 2019. "Kia Hiwa Ra: Social Anthropology in Oceania, One Maori View." *Paper Presented at the Annual Meeting of the Association for Social Anthropology in Oceania*, Auckland, New Zealand.

134

Works Cited

Bacchiddu, Giovanna. 2004. "Stepping Between Two Worlds." *Anthropology Matters Journal* 6(2):1–9.

Balasescu, Alexandru. 2007. "On the Ethnographic Subject: Multisited Research, Urban Anthropology, and Their Methods." Online: http://www.socsci.uci.edu/~eth nog/Turns/Balasescu.pdf.

Balikci, Asen. 1964. *Development of Basic Socioeconomic Units in Two Eskimo Communities*. Ottawa: National Museum of Canada, Bulletin 202.

Barad, Karen. 2007. *Meeting the Universe Halfway: Quantum Physics and the Entanglement of Matter and Meaning*. Durham: Duke University Press.

Bashkow, Ira. 2017. *The Meaning of White Men: Race and Modernity in the Orokaiva Cultural World*. Chicago: University of Chicago Press.

Bateson, Gregory. 1936. *Naven: A Survey of the Problems Suggested by a Composite Picture of the Culture of a New Guinea Tribe Drawn from Three Points of View*. Palo Alto: Stanford.

———. 1972. *Steps to an Ecology of Mind*. New York: Chandler.

Behar, Ruth. 1997. *The Vulnerable Observer: Anthropology that Breaks Your Heart*. Boston: Beacon Press.

———. 1993. "Women Writing Culture: Another Telling of the Story of American Anthropology." *Critique of Anthropology* 13(4):307–25.

Behar, Ruth and Deborah A. Gordon, eds. 1995. *Women Writing Culture*. Berkeley: University of California Press.

Bell, Joshua. 2017. "A Bundle of Relations: Collections, Collecting, and Communities." *Annual Review of Anthropology* 46:241–59.

Bell, Sandra and Simon Coleman, eds. 1999. *The Anthropology of Friendship*: *Enduring Themes and Future Possibilities*. Oxford: Berg.

Bentz, Marilyn. 1997. "Beyond Ethics: Science, Friendship, and Privacy." In *Indians and Anthropologists*: *Vine Deloria, Jr. and the Critique of Anthropology*, edited by Thomas Biosli and Larry L. Zimmerman, pp. 120–32. Tucson: The University of Arizona Press.

Bernard, H. Russell. 2011. *Research Methods in Anthropology: Qualitative and Quantitative Approaches*. New York: Rowman & Littlefield.

Bibeau, Gilles. 1997. "At Work in the Fields of Public Health: The Abuse of Rationality." *Medical Anthropology Quarterly* 11(2):246–55.

Biruk, Crystal. 2017. "Ethical Gifts? An Analysis of Soap-for-Data Transactions in Malawian Survey Research Worlds." *Medical Anthropology Quarterly* 31(3):365–84.

Bollier, David and Silke Helfrich, eds. 2015. *Patterns of Commoning*. New York: Commons Strategy Group and Off the Common Press.

Boltanski, Luc. 1999. *Distant Suffering: Morality, Media and Politics*. Translator Graham D. Burchell. Cambridge: Cambridge University Press.

Bowen, Eleanor Smith [Lauren Bohannan]. 1964. *Return to Laughter: An Anthropological Novel*. New York: Dover.

Brandes, Stanley. 1984. "Animal Metaphors and Social Control in Tzintzuntzan." *Ethnology* 23(3):207–15.

Briggs, Jean. 1970. *Never in Anger: Portrait of an Eskimo Family*. Cambridge: Harvard University Press.

———. 1986. "Kapluna Daughter." In *Women in the Field*, edited by Peggy Golde, pp. 19–46. Berkeley: University of California Press.

Brown, Karen McCarthy. 2001. *Mama Lola: A Vodou Priestess in Brooklyn*. Berkeley: University of California Press.

Bruner, Edward. 1999. "Return to Sumatra: 1957–1997. *American Ethnologist* 26(2): 461–77.

Calderon, Dolores. 2016. "Moving from Damage-Centered Research through Unsettling Reflexivity." *Anthropology and Education Quarterly* 47(1):5–24.

Campbell, Will D. 1977. *Brother to a Dragonfly*. New York: The Seabury Press.

———. 1986. *Forty Acres and a Goat*. Jackson: University Press of Mississippi.

Carrier, James G. 1999. "People Who Can Be Friends: Selves and Social Relationships." In *The Anthropology of Friendship: Enduring Themes and Future Possibilities*, edited by Sandra Bell and Simon Coleman, pp. 21–38. Oxford: Berg.

Carvalho, Clara. 2012. "Guinean Migrant Traditional Healers in the Global Market." In *Medicine, Mobility, and Power in Global Africa*, edited by Hansjörg Dilger, Abdoulaye Kane, and Stacey A. Langwick, pp. 316–36. Bloomington: Indiana University Press.

Cassell, Joan. 1980. "Ethical Principles for Conducting Fieldwork." *American Anthropologist* 82:28–41.

Cesara, Manda [Karla Poewe]. 1982. *Reflections of a Woman Anthropologist*. London: Academic Press.

Chabal, Patrick and Toby Green, eds. 2016. *Guinea-Bissau: Micro-state to 'Narco-State'*. London: Hurst & Company.

Chen, Mel Y. 2012. *Animacies: Biopolitics, Racial Mattering, and Queer Affect*. Durham: Duke University Press.

Chilisa, Bagele. 2012. *Indigenous Research Methodologies*. Thousand Oaks: SAGE Publications.

Coe, Cati. 2005. *Dilemmas of Culture in African Schools: Youth, Nationalism, and the Transformation of Knowledge*. Chicago: University of Chicago Press.

Coleman, Simon. 2006. "The Multi-Sited Ethnographer." In *Critical Journeys: The Making of Anthropologists*, edited by Geert de Neve and Maya Unnithan-Kumar, pp. 31–46. Burlington: Ashgate.

Collins, Patricia Hill. 1998. *Fighting Words: Black Women and the Search for Justice*. Minneapolis: University of Minnesota Press.

Counts, David R. and Dorothy Ayers Counts. 1998. "Fictive Families in the Field." In *Fieldwork and Families: Constructing New Models for Ethnographic Research*, edited by Juliana Flinn, Leslie Marshall, and Jocelyn Armstrong, pp. 142–53. Honolulu: University of Hawai'i Press.

Cross, Jamie. 2014. "The Coming of the Corporate Gift." *Theory, Culture, and Society* 31(2/3):121–45.

Cummings, Maggie. 2013. "Afterword: Expertise in Our Time." *Anthropologica* 55(2):329–34.

D'Alisera, JoAnn. 2004. *An Imagined Geography: Sierra Leonean Muslims in America*. Philadelphia: University of Pennsylvania Press.

Davies, James and Dimitrina Spencer, eds. 2010. *Emotions in the Field: The Psychology and Anthropology of Fieldwork Experiences.* Stanford: Stanford University Press.

Deloria, Vine, Jr. 1969. *Custer Died for Your Sins: An Indian Manifesto.* New York: Macmillan.

Denzin, Norman, Yvonna Lincoln, and Linda Tuhiwai Smith, eds. 2008. *Handbook of Critical and Indigenous Methodologies.* Thousand Oaks: SAGE Publications.

DeVita, Philip R., ed. 1990. *The Humbled Anthropologist: Tales from the Pacific.* Belmont: Wadsworth Publishing Company.

Donnelly, John. 2012. *A Twist of Faith: An American Christian's Quest to Help Orphans in Africa.* Boston: Beacon Press.

Douglas, Mary. 1957. "Animals in Lele Religious Symbolism." *Africa* 27(1):46–58.

Duclos, Diane. 2019. "When Ethnography Does Not Rhyme with Anonymity: Reflections on Name Disclosure, Self-Censorship, and Storytelling." *Ethnography* 20(2):175–83.

Dumont, Louis. 1986. *Essays on Individualism: Modern Ideology in Anthropological Perspective.* Chicago: University of Chicago Press.

Dutheil, April, Frank Tester, and Jordan Konek. 2015. "Unequal Exchange: Western Economic Logic and Inuit/Qablunaat Research Relationships." *Polar Record* 51(2):140–50.

Dyck, Noel and James B. Waldram, eds. 1993. *Anthropology, Public Policy, and Native Peoples in Canada.* Montreal: McGill-Queen's Press.

Easterly, William. 2006. *The White Man's Burden: Why the West's Efforts to Aid the Rest Have Done So Much Ill and So Little Good.* New York: Oxford University Press.

Englund, Harri. 1996. "Witchcraft, Modernity and the Person: The Morality of Accumulation in Central Malawi." *Critique of Anthropology* 16(3):257–79.

Escobar, Arturo. 1995. *Encountering Development: The Making and Unmaking of the Third World.* Princeton: Princeton University Press.

———. 2018. *Designs for the Pluriverse: Radical Interdependence, Autonomy, and the Making of Worlds.* Durham: Duke University Press.

Evans-Pritchard, E.E. 1937. *Witchcraft, Oracles and Magic among the Azande.* Oxford: Clarendon.

Falzon, M.A., ed. 2016 [2009]. *Multi-sited Ethnography, Theory, Praxis and Locality in Contemporary Research.* London: Routledge.

Federici, Sylvia. 2004. *Caliban and the Witch: Women, the Body and Primitive Accumulation.* New York: Autonomedia.

Feld, Steven. 2012. *Jazz Cosmopolitanism in Accra: Five Musical Years in Ghana.* Durham: Duke University Press.

Ferguson, James. 1994. *The Anti-Politics Machine: "Development," Depoliticization, and Bureaucratic Power in Lesotho.* Minneapolis: University of Minnesota Press.

———. 2006. *Global Shadows: Africa in the Neoliberal World Order.* Durham: Duke University Press.

Fernea, Elizabeth Warnock. [1965]1989. *Guests of the Sheik: An Ethnography of an Iraqi Village.* New York: Anchor Books.

Fienup-Riordan, Ann. 2000. "What's in a Name? Becoming a Real Person in a Yup'ik Community." In *Hunting Tradition in a Changing World*, edited by Ann Fienup Riordan, William Tyson, Paul John, Marie Meade, and John Active, pp. 183–200. New Brunswick: Rutgers University Press.

Fisher, Josh. 2010. "Building Consciousness: The Organization Workshop Comes to a Nicaraguan Cooperative." *Anthropology of Work Review* 31(2):71–82.

———. 2013. "Fair or Balanced? The Other Side of Fair Trade in a Nicaraguan Sewing Cooperative." *Anthropological Quarterly* 86(2):527–58.

———. 2017. "The Unemployed Cooperative: Community Responses to Joblessness in Nicaragua." in *Anthropologies of Unemployment: The Changing Study of Work and its Absence*, edited by. C. Lane and J.B. Kwon, pp. 191–211 Ithaca: Cornell University Press.

———. 2018. "In Search of Dignified Work: Gender and the Work Ethic in the Crucible of Fair Trade Production." *American Ethnologist* 45(1):74–86.

Fisher, Josh and Alex Nading. n.d. "Ethnographic Designs for Living Well Together: Notes from an Experiment in Collaboration." *Unpublished manuscript.*

Flinn, Julianna. 1990. "Reflections of a Shy Ethnographer: Foot-in-the-Mouth Is Not Fatal." In *The Humbled Anthropologist: Tales from the Pacific*, edited by Philip R. DeVita, pp. 46–52. Belmont: Wadsworth Publishing Company.

Flinn, Juliana, Leslie Marshall, and Jocelyn Armstrong, eds. 1998. *Fieldwork and Families: Constructing New Models for Ethnographic Research.* Honolulu: University of Hawai'i Press.

Fluehr-Lobban, Carolyn. 2003a. "Dialogue for Ethically Conscious Practice." In *Ethics and the Profession of Anthropology*, edited by Carolyn Fleuhr-Lobban, 2nd edition, pp. 225–46. Walnut Creek: Altamira Press.

Fluehr-Lobban, Carolyn, ed. 2003b. *Ethics and the Profession of Anthropology*, 2nd edition. Walnut Creek: Altamira Press.

Forrest, Joshua. 1992. *Guinea-Bissau: Power, Conflict, and Renewal in a West African Nation.* Boulder: Westview Press.

Fourshey, Catherine Cymone. 2012. Karibu Stranger, Come Heal Thy Host: Hospitality as Historical Subject in Southwestern Tanzania, 1600-1900. *African Historical Review* 44(2):18–54.

Freeman, Milton M.R., ed. 1976. *Report, Inuit Land Use and Occupancy Project,* 3 Vols. Ottawa: Department of Indian Affairs and Northern Development.

Friere, Paolo. 2000. *Pedagogy of the Oppressed.* New York: Bloomsbury.

Gay y Blasco, Paloma and Liria Hernández. 2020. *Writing Friendship: A Reciprocal Ethnography.* London: Palgrave Macmillan.

Geertz, Clifford. 1988. *Works and Lives: The Anthropologist as Author.* Stanford: Stanford University Press.

———. 2000. *Available Light.* Princeton: Princeton University Press.

Geertz, Hildred and Clifford Geertz. 1964. "Teknonymy in Bali: Parenthood, Age-grading and Genealogical Amnesia." *Man* 94(2):94–108.

Gibson-Graham, J.K. 1996. *The End of Capitalism (As We Knew It): A Feminist Critique of Political Economy.* Minneapolis: University of Minnesota Press.

———. 2006. *A Postcapitalist Politics.* Minneapolis: University of Minnesota Press.

Gilroy, Paul. 1991. *There Ain't No Black in the Union Jack: The Cultural Politics of Race and Nation.* Chicago: University of Chicago Press.

———. 1993. *The Black Atlantic: Modernity and Double Consciousness.* New York: Verso.

Goldberg, Susan. 2018. "For Decades, Our Coverage Was Racist. To Rise above Our Past, We Must Acknowledge It." *National Geographic.* April Special Issue, pp.4–6.

Gombay, Nicole. 2009. "Sharing or Commoditizing? A Discussion of the Some of the Socio-economic Implications of Nunavik's Hunter Support Program." *Polar Record* 45(233):119–32.

———. 2010. *Making a Living: Place, Food, and Economy in an Inuit Community.* Saskatoon: Purich Publishing Limited.

Gottlieb, Alma. 1986. "Dog: Ally or Traitor? Mythology, Cosmology, and Society among the Beng of Ivory Coast." *American Ethnologist* 13(3):477–88.

———. 1995. "Beyond the Lonely Anthropologist: Collaboration in Research and Writing." *American Anthropologist* 97(1):21–6.

———. 2004. *"The Afterlife is Where We Come From": The Culture of Infant Care in West Africa.* Chicago: University of Chicago Press.

———. 2012a. "Two Visions of Africa: Reflections on Fieldwork in an 'Animist Bush' and in an Urban Diaspora." In *The Restless Anthropologist: New Fieldsites, New Visions,* edited by Alma Gottlieb, pp. 81–99. Chicago: University of Chicago Press.

———, ed. 2012b. *The Restless Anthropologist: New Fieldsites, New Visions.* Chicago: University of Chicago Press.

———. 2018. "Processing Privilege: Reflections on Fieldwork (Early, and otherwise) among Beng Villagers of Cote d'Ivoire." *Mande Studies* 20:123–35.

Gottlieb, Alma and Philip Graham. 1993. *Parallel Worlds: An Anthropologist and a Writer Encounter Africa.* Chicago: University of Chicago Press.

———. 1999. "Revising the Text, Revisioning the Field: Reciprocity over the Long Term. *Anthropology and Humanism* 24(2): 117–28.

———. 2012. *Braided Worlds.* Chicago: University of Chicago Press.

Goulet, Jean-Guy and Bruce Granville Miller, eds. 2007. *Extraordinary Anthropology: Transformations in the Field.* Lincoln: University of Nebraska Press.

Graeber, David. 2009. *Debt: The First Five Thousand Years.* Brooklyn: Melville House.

Graburn, Nelson. 1969. *Eskimos without Igloos: Social and Economic Development in Sugluk.* Boston: Little Brown and Company.

Grindal, Bruce and Frank A. Salamone, eds. 2006 [1995], *Bridges to Humanity: Narratives on Fieldwork and Friendship,* 2nd edition. Long Grove: Waveland.

Gudeman, Stephen F. 2001. *The Anthropology of Economy: Community, Market, and Culture.* Malden: Blackwell.

Handman, Courtney. 2017. "Walking Like a Christian: Roads, Translation, and Gendered Bodies as Religious Infrastructure in Papua New Guinea." *American Ethnologist* 44(2):315–27.

Hannerz, Ulf. 2003. "Being There... and There... and There! Reflections on Multi-Site Ethnography." *Ethnography* 4(1):201–16.

Haraway, Donna. 1988. "Situated Knowledges: The Science Question in Feminism and the Privilege of Partial Perspective." *Feminist Studies* 14(3):575–99.

———. 2008. *When Species Meet.* Minneapolis: University of Minnesota Press.

———. 2016. *Staying with the Trouble: Making Kin in the Chthulucene.* Durham: Duke University Press.

Harder, Miriam T. and George Wenzel. 2012. "Inuit Subsistence, Social Economy and Food Security in Clyde River, Nunavut." *Arctic* 65(3):305–18.

Hardin, Jessica, and Christina Ting Kwauk. 2019. "Elemental Eating: Samoan Public Health and Valuation in Health Promotion." *The Contemporary Pacific* 31(2): 381–415.

Hartsock, Nancy. 1983. *Money, Sex, and Power: Toward a Feminist Historical Materialism.* Boston: Northeastern University Press.

Hau'Ofa, Epeli. 1994. "Our Sea of Islands." *The Contemporary Pacific* 6(1):147–61.

Hess, Sabine. 2011. "Learning How to Relate: Notes of a Female Anthropologist on Working with a Male Fieldworker in Vanuatu. In *Working Together in Vanuatu: Research Histories, Collaborations, Projects and Reflections*, edited by John P. Taylor and Nick Thieberger, pp. 217–22. Canberra: ANU Press.

Holsey, Bayo. 2013. "Black Atlantic Visions: History, Race, and Transnationalism in Ghana." *Cultural Anthropology* 28(3): 504–18.

Hough, Caroline, with Daria Izdebska, eds. 2016. *The Oxford Handbook of Names and Naming.* Oxford: Oxford University Press.

Howell, Nancy. 1990. *Surviving Fieldwork.* Washington, D.C.: American Anthropological Association.

Howell, Signe and Aud Talle. 2012a. Introduction. In *Returns to the Field*, edited by Signe Howell and Aud Talle, pp. 1–22. Bloomington: Indiana University Press.

———, eds. 2012b. *Returns to the Field: Multitemporal Research and Contemporary Anthropology.* Bloomington: Indiana University Press.

Hume, Lynne and Jane Mulcock, eds. 2004. A*nthropologists in the Field: Cases in Participant Observation.* New York: Columbia University Press.

Hutchinson, Sharon E. 1996. *Nuer Dilemmas: Coping with Money, War, and the State.* Berkeley: University of California Press.

Ice, Gillian H., Darna L. Dufour and Nancy J. Stevens. 2015. *Disasters in Field Research: Preparing for and Coping with Unexpected Events.* Lanham: Rowman & Littlefield.

Ingold, Tim. 2011. *Being Alive: Essays on Movement, Knowledge, and Description.* New York: Routledge.

Janes, Craig R. and Kitty K. Corbett. 2009. "Anthropology and Global Health." *Annual Review of Anthropology* 38:167–83.

Johnson, Michelle C. 2000. "Becoming a Muslim; Become a Person: Female 'Circumcision,' Religious Identity, and Personhood in Guinea-Bissau." In *Female "Circumcision" in Africa: Culture, Controversy, and Change*, edited by Bettina Shell-Duncan and Ylva Hernlund, pp. 215–33. Boulder: Lynne Rienner Publishers.

———. 2013. "Culture's Calling: Mobile Phones and the Making of an African Migrant Village in Lisbon." *Anthropology Quarterly* 86(1): 163–90.

————. 2014. "Guinea-Bissau." In *Worldmark Encyclopedia of Religious Practices*, edited by. Thomas Riggs, 2nd edition, Vol. 3: Countries: Greece to Philippines, pp. 40–49. Detroit: Gale.

————. 2016. "'Nothing Is Sweet in My Mouth': Food, Identity, and Religion in African Lisbon." *Food and Foodways* 24(3–4): 234–56.

————. 2017. "Never Forget Where You're From: Raising Guinean Muslim Babies in Portugal." In *A World of Babies: Imagined Childcare Guides for Eight Societies*, edited by Alma Gottlieb and Judy DeLoache, 2nd edition, pp. 33–70. Cambridge: Cambridge University Press.

————. 2020. *Remaking Islam in African Portugal: Lisbon – Mecca – Bissau*. Bloomington: Indiana University Press.

Jolles, Carol Zane. 2002. *Faith, Food, and Family in a Yupik Whaling Community*. Seattle: University of Washington Press.

————. 2006. "Listening to Elders, Working with Youth." In *Critical Inuit Studies*, edited by Pamela Stern and Lisa Stevenson, pp. 35–53. Lincoln: University of Nebraska Press.

Jolly, Margaret. 2007. "Imagining Oceania: Indigenous and Foreign Representations of a Sea of Islands." *The Contemporary Pacific* 19(2):508–45.

Kan, Sergei, ed. 2001. *Stranger to Relatives: The Adoption and Naming of Anthropologists in Native North America*. Lincoln: University of Nebraska Press.

Karetak, Joe, Frank Tester, and Shirley Tagalik, eds. 2017. *Inuit Qaujimajatuqangit: What Inuit Have Always Known to Be True*. Halifax: Fernwood Publishing. Kindle Edition.

Karim, Lamia. 2011. *Microfinance and Its Discontents: Women in Debt in Bangladesh*. Minneapolis: University of Minnesota Press.

Keller, Janet Dixon and Takaronga Kuautonga. 2008. *Nokonofo Kitea (We Keep on Living this Way): Myths and Music of Futuna, Vanuatu*. Honolulu: University of Hawai'i Press.

Kemmis, Stephen and Robin McTaggart. 2005. "Participatory Action Research: Communicative Action and the Public Sphere." In *The Sage Handbook of Qualitative Research*, edited by Norman Denzin and Yvonna Lincoln, 3rd edition, pp. 559–603. Thousand Oaks: SAGE Publications.

Kim, Esther Chihye. 2009. "'Mama's Family': Fictive Kinship and Undocumented Immigrant Restaurant Workers." *Ethnography* 10(4):497–513.

Kingston, Sean, Alma Gottlieb and Jonathan Benthall. 1997. "Gift Relationships Between Ethnographers and Their Hosts." *Anthropology Today* 13(6):27–8.

Kirsch, Stuart. 2018. *Engaged Anthropology: Politics beyond the Text*. Berkeley: University of California Press.

Knauft, Bruce. 2009. *The Gebusi: Lives Transformed in a Rainforest World*. New York: McGraw-Hill.

————. 2012. "Afterword: Reflecting on Returns to the Field." In *Returns to the Field: Multitemporal Research and Contemporary Anthropology*, edited by Signe Howell and Aud Talle, pp. 250–60, Bloomington: Indiana University Press.

Kockelman, Paul. 2013. *Agent, Person, Subject, Self: A Theory of Ontology, Interaction, and Infrastructure*. Oxford: Oxford University Press.

Konner, Melvin and Sarah H. Davis, eds. 2011. *Being There: Learning to Live Cross-Culturally*. Cambridge: Harvard University Press.

Kovach, Margaret. 2010. *Indigenous Methodologies: Characteristics, Conversations, and Contexts*. Toronto: University of Toronto Press.

Kral, Michael and Lori Idlout. 2006. "Participatory Anthropology in Nunavut." In *Critical Inuit Studies*, edited by Pamela Stern and Lisa Stevenson, pp. 54–70. Lincoln: University of Nebraska Press.

Lassiter, Luke E. 2005a. *The Chicago Guide to Collaborative Ethnography*. Chicago: University of Chicago Press.

———. 2005b. "Collaborative Ethnography and Public Anthropology." *Current Anthropology* 46(1):83–106.

Lather, Patti. 2001. "Postbook: Working the Ruins of Feminist Ethnography." *Signs: Journal of Women in Culture and Society* 27(1):199–227.

Leach, Edmund. 1964. "Anthropological Aspects of Language: Animal Categories and Verbal Abuse." In *New directions in the study of language*, edited by E.H. Lenneberg, pp. 23–63. Boston: MIT Press.

Lederman, Rena. 2016. "Fieldwork Double-Bound in Human Research Ethics Reviews: Disciplinary Competence, or Regulatory Compliance and the Muting of Disciplinary Values." In *The Ethics Rupture: Exploring Alternatives to Formal Research-Ethics Review*, edited by Will C. van den Hoonaard and Ann Hamilton, pp. 43–72. Toronto: University of Toronto Press.

Lee, Molly. 2006. "Flora and me." In *Critical Inuit Studies*, edited by Pamela Stern and Lisa Stevenson, pp. 25–34. Lincoln: University of Nebraska Press.

Levine, Nancy E. 2008. "Alternative Kinship, Marriage, and Reproduction," *Annual Review of Anthropology* 37:375–89.

Levins, Richard and Richard Lewontin. 1985. *The Dialectical Biologist*. Cambridge: Harvard University Press.

Levi-Strauss, Claude. 1952. *Race and History*. Paris: UNESCO.

———. 1964 [1962]. *Totemism*. Rodney Needham, transl. London: Merlin Press.

———. 1966 [1962]. "The Individual as a Species." in *The Savage Mind*, edited by Claude Lévi-Strauss, Transl. anon, pp. 191–216. Chicago: University of Chicago Press.

———. 1969 [1949]. *The Elementary Structures of Kinship*. Rodney Needham, transl. London: Eyre and Spottiswoode.

Machado, Fernando Luis. 1998. "Da Guiné-Bissau a Portugal: Luso-Guineenses e Imigrantes." *Sociologia: Problemas e Practicas* 26:9–56.

Malinowski, Bronislaw. 1984 [1922]. *Argonauts of the Western Pacific: An Account of Native Enterprise and Adventure in the Archipelagoes of Melanesian New Guinea*. Prospect Heights: Waveland Press.

Marcus, George. 1998 [1995]. "Ethnography in/of the World System: The Emergence of Multi-Sited Ethnography." In *Ethnography through Thick and Thin*, edited by George Marcus, pp. 79–104. Princeton: Princeton University Press.

Matory, James Lorand. 2015. *Stigma and Culture: Last-Place Anxiety in Black Culture*. Chicago: University of Chicago Press.

Maturana, Humberto and Francisco Varela. 1987. *The Tree of Knowledge: The Biological Roots of Human Understanding*. Boston: Shambhala.

Mauss, Marcel. 2016 [1925]. *The Gift: The Form and Reason for Exchange in Archaic Societies.* Chicago: HAU Books.

Mbembe, Achille. 2017. *The Critique of Black Reason.* Durham: Duke University Press.

McElroy, Ann. 2008. *Nunavut Generations.* Long Grove: Waveland Press.

McKinnon, Susan and Sarah Franklin. 2000. "New Directions in Kinship Study: A Core Concept Revisited." *Current Anthropology* 41(2): 275–78.

McLean, Athena and Annette Leibing, eds. 2007. *The Shadow Side of Fieldwork: Exploring the Blurred Borders between Ethnography and Life.* Oxford: Blackwell Publishing.

McNabb, Steven. 1993. "Commentary." *Human Organization* 52(2): 216–24.

Mendy, Peter Karibe and Richard Lobban Jr. 2013. *The Historical Dictionary of the Republic of Guinea-Bissau,* 4th edition. Plymouth: Scarecrow Press, Inc.

Miller, Jay. 2001. "Naming as Humanizing." In *Strangers to Relatives: The Adoption and Naming of Anthropologists in Native North America*, edited by Sergei Kan, pp. 141–58. Lincoln: University of Nebraska Press.

Mintz, Sidney W. 2000 "Sows' Ears and Silver Linings: A Backward Look at Ethnography." *Current Anthropology* 41(2):169–89.

Mommersteeg, Geert. 2012. *In the City of the Marabouts: Islamic Culture in West Africa.* Long Grove: Waveland Press.

Moreno, Eva [pseudonym]. 1995. "Rape in the Field: Reflections from a Survivor." In *Taboo: Sex, Identity, and Erotic Subjectivity in Anthropological Fieldwork*, edited by Don Kulick and Margaret Willson, pp. 219–50. London: Routledge.

Moyo, Dambisa. 2009. *Dead Aid: Why Aid Is Not Working and How There Is a Better Way for Africa.* New York: Farrar, Straus and Giroux.

Munk, Nina. 2013. *The Idealist: Jeffrey Sachs and the Quest to End Poverty.* New York: Anchor Books.

Nancy, Jean-Luc. 1991. *The Inoperative Community.* Minneapolis: University of Minnesota Press.

Narayan, Kirin. 1993. "How Native is the 'Native' Anthropologist?" *American Anthropologist* 95(3):671–86.

Nourse, Jennifer. 2002. "Who's Exploiting Whom: Agency, Fieldwork, and Representation among Lauje of Indonesia. *Anthropology and Humanism.* 27(1):27–42.

Nuttall, Mark. 2000. "Choosing Kin in a Greenlandic Community." In *Dividends of Kinship*, edited by Peter P. Schweitzer, pp. 33–60. New York: Routledge.

Nuttall, Mark, Fikret Berkes, Bruce Forbes, Gary Kofinas, Tatiana Vlassova and George Wenzel. 2005. "Hunting, Herding, Fishing, and Gathering: Indigenous Peoples and Renewable Resource Use in the Arctic." In *Arctic Climate Impact Assessment. ACIA Overview Report*, ed. Carolyn Symon, Lelani Arris, and Bill Heal, pp. 649–90. New York: Cambridge University Press.

Ortiz, Simon. 2002. *Out There Somewhere.* Tucson: University of Arizona Press.

Ostrom, Elinor. *1990. Governing the Commons: The Evolution of Institutions for Collective* Action. Cambridge: Cambridge University Press.

Patterson, Diana. 2012. "Fictive Kinship and the Anthropologist's Position." In *Anthropologies: Collaborative Online Project* 9 (special issue: Kinship in the 21st Century). Online: http://www.anthropologiesproject.org/2012/04/fictive-kinship -and-anthropologists.html.

Pfeiffer, James and Rachel Chapman. 2010. "Anthropological Perspectives on Structural Adjustment and Public Health." *Annual Review of Anthropology* 39:149–65.

Pierre, Jemima. 2013. *The Predicament of Blackness in Post-colonial Ghana.* Chicago: Chicago University Press.

———. 2020. "The Racial Vernaculars of Development: A View from West Africa." *American Anthropologist* 122(1):86–98.

Pink, Sarah. 1998. "The White 'Helpers': Anthropologists, Development Workers and Local Imaginations." *Anthropology Today* 14(6):9–14.

Piot, Charles. 1999. *Remotely Global: Village Modernity in West Africa.* Durham: Duke University Press.

Powdermaker, Hortense. 1966. *Stranger and Friend: The Way of the Anthropologist.* New York: Norton.

Ready, Elspeth and Eleanor A. Power. 2018. "Why Wage Earners Hunt: Food Sharing, Social Structure, and Influence in an Arctic Mixed Economy." *Current Anthropology* 59(1):74–97.

Ribeiro, Eduardo and Arturo Escobar. 2015. "Red de Antropologías del Mundo: Intervenciones en la Imaginación Teórica y Política de la Práctica Antropológica." In *Prácticas Otras de Conocimiento(s): Entre Crisis, entre Guerra*, edited by X. Leyva, pp. 381–402. Guadalajara: Editorial Retos.

Rist, Gilbert. 2002. *The History of Development: From Western Origins to Global Faith.* New York: Zed Books.

Robinson, Gary. 2004 "Living in Sheds: Suicide, Friendship, and Research among the Tiwi." In *Anthropologists in the Field: Cases in Participant Observation*, edited by Lynne Hume and Jane Mulcock, pp. 153–67. New York: Columbia University Press.

Rodman, William and Margaret Rodman. 1990. "To Die on Ambae: On the Possibility of Doing Fieldwork Forever." In *The Humbled Anthropologist: Tales from the Pacific*, edited by Philip R. DeVita, pp. 101–20. Belmont: Wadsworth Publishing Company.

Roelvink, Gerda, Kevin St Martin and J.K. Gibson-Graham. 2015. *Making Other Worlds Possible: Performing Diverse Economies.* Minneapolis: University of Minnesota Press.

Rouse, Carolyn. 2014. "Don't Let the Lion Tell the Giraffe's Story: Law, Violence, and Ontological Insecurities in Ghana." In *Bioinsecurity and Vulnerability*, edited by Nancy N. Chen and Leslie A. Sharp, pp. 121–42. Santa Fe: SAR Press.

———. 2019. "Claude Levi-Strauss's Contribution to the Race Question: *Race and History. American Anthropologist* 121(3):721–24.

Royce, Anya Peterson. 2017. "Elizabeth Colson (1917-2016): Reflections on a Conversation." *Anthropology Southern Africa* 40(2):142–6.

————. 2016. *Prestigio y Afiliación de una Comunidad Urbana: Juchitán, Oaxaca.* Colección Xhono Gui'Chi'. Juchitán: Fundación Excellentiam.

————. 2011. *Becoming an Ancestor: The Isthmus Zapotec Way of Death.* Albany: SUNY Press.

————. 2002. "Learning to See, Learning to Listen: Thirty-Five Years of Fieldwork with the Isthmus Zapotec." In *Chronicling Cultures: Long-Term Field Research in Anthropology,* edited by Robert V. Kemper and Anya Peterson Royce, pp. 8–33. Walnut Creek: AltaMira Press.

Royce, Anya Peterson and Robert V. Kemper. 2002. "Long-Term Field Research: Metaphors, Paradigms, and Themes." In *Chronicling Cultures: Long-Term Field Research in Anthropology,* edited by Robert V. Kemper and Anya Peterson Royce, pp. xiii–xxxviii. Walnut Creek: AltaMira Press.

Samudra, Jaida Kim. 2015. "Attacked in the Field: Encountering a Street Gang While Studying Peace in Java." In *At Home and in the Field: Ethnographic Encounters in Asia and the Pacific Islands,* edited by Suzanne S. Finney, Mary Mostafanezhad, Guido Carlo Pigliasco, and Forrest Wade Young, pp. 18–23. Honolulu: University of Hawai'i Press.

Schensul, Stephen L., Jean J. Schensul and Margaret LeCompte. 1999. *Essential Ethnographic Methods: Observations, Interviews, and Questionnaires.* New York: Rowman & Littlefield.

Schneider, David M. 1980 [1968]. *American Kinship: A Cultural Account.* Revised, 2nd edition. Chicago: University of Chicago Press.

————. 1997. "The Power of Culture: Notes on Some Aspects of Gay and Lesbian Kinship in America Today." *Cultural Anthropology* 12 (2):269–73.

Scott, James C. 1985. *Weapons of the Weak: Everyday Forms of Peasant Resistance.* New Haven: Yale University Press.

Searles, Edmund. 2002. "Food and the Making of Modern Inuit Identities." *Food and Foodways* 10(1–2):55–78.

————. 2010. "Placing Identity: Town, Land, and Authenticity in Nunavut, Canada." *Acta Borealia* 27(2):151–66.

————. 2016. "To Sell or Not to Sell: Country Food Markets and Inuit Identity in Nunavut." *Food and Foodways* 24(3–4):194–212.

Shirk, Jennifer L., Heidi L. Ballard, Candie C. Wilderman, Tina Phillips, Andrea Wiggins, Rebecca Jordan, Ellen McCallie, Matthew Minarchek, Bruce V. Lewenstein, Marianne E. Krasny and Rick Bonney. 2012. "Public Participation in Scientific Research: A Framework for Deliberate Design." *Ecology and Society* 17(2):29–49.

Simpson, Peter L.P. 2013. *The Eudemian Ethics of Aristotle.* Somerset: Routledge. Accessed July 9, 2018. ProQuest Ebook Central.

Singer, Merrill. 1994. "Community-Centered Praxis: Toward an Alternative non-dominative Applied Anthropology." *Human Organization* 53(4):336–44.

Small, Cathy A. 1997. *Voyages: From Tongan Villages to American Suburbs.* Ithaca: Cornell University Press.

Smith, Linda Tuhiwai. 2012. *Decolonizing Methodologies: Research and Indigenous Peoples.* London: Zed Books.

Smucker, Thomas A., David J. Campbell, Jennifer M. Olson and Elizabeth E. Wangui. 2016. "Contemporary Challenges of Participatory Field Research for Land Use Change Analyses: Examples from Kenya." *Field Methods* 19(4):384–406.

Sontag, Susan. 2004. *Regarding the Pain of Others*. London: Penguin Books.

Spivak, Gayatri. 1999. *A Critique of Postcolonial Reason: Toward a History of the Vanishing Present.* Cambridge: Harvard University Press.

Statistics Canada. 2017. *Nunavut [Territory] and Canada [Country]* (Table). *Census Profile.*2016 Census. Statistics Canada Catalogue No. 98-316-X2016001. Ottawa. Released November 29, 2017. https://www12.statcan.gc.ca/census-recensement /2016/dp-pd/prof/index.cfm?Lang=E. Accessed July 17, 2018.

Stengers, Isabelle and Ilya Prigogine. 1984. *Order Out of Chaos: Man's New Dialogue with Nature.* New York: Bantam.

Stevenson, Lisa. 2006. "Introduction." In *Critical Inuit Studies*, edited by Pamela Stern and Lisa Stevenson, pp. 1–22. Lincoln: University of Nebraska Press.

Stoller, Paul. 1989. *The Taste of Ethnographic Things: The Senses in Anthropology.* Philadelphia: University of Pennsylvania Press.

———. 2016. "Writing for the Future," In *The Anthropologist as Writer,* edited by Helena Wulff, pp. 118–28. New York: Berghahn Books.

Stoller, Paul and Cheryl Olkes. 1987. *In Sorcery's Shadow: A Memoir of Apprenticeship among the Songhay of Niger.* Chicago: University of Chicago Press.

Strathern, Andrew. 1983. "Research in Papua New Guinea, Cross-Currents of Conflict." *RAIN* 58:4–10.

Strathern, Marilyn. 1988. *The Gender of the Gift: Problems with Women and Problems with Society in Melanesia.* Berkeley: University of California Press.

———. 1999. *Property, Substance and Effect: Anthropological Essays on Persons and Things.* London: Althone Press.

Straus, Ann S. 2001. "Tell Your Sister to Come Eat." In *Strangers to Relatives: The Adoption and Naming of Anthropologists in Native North America*, edited by Sergei Kan, pp. 175–84. Lincoln: University of Nebraska Press.

Tambiah, S.J. 1969. "Animals Are Good to Think and Good to Prohibit." *Ethnology* 8(4):423–59.

Taussig, Michael. 1980. *The Devil and Commodity Fetishism in South America.* Chapel Hill: University of North Carolina Press.

Taylor, Stephen J. 1991. "Leaving the Field: Research, Relationships, and Responsibilities." In *Experiencing Fieldwork: An Inside View of Qualitative Research*, edited by William B. Shaffir and Robert A. Stebbins, pp. 238–47. Newbury Park: SAGE Publications.

Tengan, Ty Kāwika. 2002. "(En)gendering Colonialism: Masculinities in Hawai'i and Aotearoa." *Cultural Values* 6(3):239–56.

Tengan, T., Tēvita O. Ka'ili and Rochelle Tuitagava'a Fonoti. "Genealogies: Articulating Indigenous Anthropology in/of Oceania." *Pacific Studies* 33 (2010): 139–167.

Thomson, Donald F. 1935. "The Joking Relationship and Organized Obscenity in North Queensland, *American Anthropologist* 37(3, Part 1): 460–90.

Tonkin, Elizabeth, ed. 1984. *Naming Systems. 1980 Proceedings of the American Ethnological Society.* Washington, D.C.: American Ethnological Society.

Trask, Haunani-Kay. 1991. "Natives and Anthropologists: The Colonial Struggle." *The Contemporary Pacific* 3(1):159–67.

Tuck, Eve and K. Wayne Yang. 2012. "Decolonization Is Not a Metaphor." *Decolonization: Indigeneity, Education and Society* 1(1):1–40.

UNESCO n.d. "World Inequality Database on Education." Online: https://www.education-inequalities.org/.

Uperesa, Fa'anofo Lisaclaire and Adriana María Garriga-López. 2017. "Contested Sovereignties: Puerto Rico and American Samoa." In *Sovereign Acts: Contesting Colonialism Across Indigenous Nations and Latinx America*, edited by Frances Negrón-Muntaner, pp. 39–81. Tucson: University of Arizona Press.

Usher, Peter. 1993. "Northern Development, Impact Assessment, and Social Change." In *Anthropology, Public Policy, and Native Peoples in Canada*, edited by Noel Dyck and James B. Waldram, pp. 98–130. Montreal: McGill-Queen's Press.

Van Maanen, John. 2011. *Tales of the Field: On Writing Ethnography*, 2nd edition. Chicago: University of Chicago Press.

Vitebsky, Piers. 2012. "Repeated Returns and Special Friends: From Mythic Encounter to Shared History. In *Returns to the Field*, edited by Signe Howell and Aud Talle, pp. 180–202. Bloomington: Indiana University Press.

Vom Bruck, Gabrielle and Barbara Bodenhorn, eds. 2006. *The Anthropology of Names and Naming.* Cambridge: Cambridge University Press.

Wagner, Roy. 2016 [1975]. *The Invention of Culture.* Revised, 2nd edition. Chicago: University of Chicago Press.

Wagoner, Gail. n.d. "Briefing Paper on Remuneration to Subject Populations and Individuals." Accessed on July 8, 2020. https://www.americananthro.org/ParticipateAndAdvocate/Content.aspx?ItemNumber=13141.

Waring, Marilyn. 1988. *Counting for Nothing: What Men Value and What Women are Worth.* Sydney: Allen & Unwin Press.

Wentworth, Chelsea. 2016. "Public Eating, Private Pain: Children, Feasting and Food Security in Vanuatu." *Food and Foodways* 24(3–4):136–52.

———. 2017. "Good Food, Bad Food, and White Rice: Understanding Child Feeding Using Visual Narrative Elicitation." *Medical Anthropology* 36(6) 602–14.

———. 2019. "Unhealthy Aid: Food Security Programming and Disaster Responses to Cyclone Pam in Vanuatu." *Anthropological Forum* 1–18.

Wenzel, George. 1991. *Animal Rights, Human Rights: Ecology, Economy, and Ideology in the Canadian Arctic.* Toronto: University of Toronto Press.

———. 1995. "Ningiqtuq: Resource Sharing and Generalized Reciprocity in Clyde River, Nunavut." *Arctic Anthropology* 32(2): 43–60.

———. 2000. "Sharing, Money, and Modern Subsistence: Obligations and Reciprocity at Clyde River, Nunavut." In *The Social Economy of Sharing: Resource Allocation and Modern Hunter-Gatherers*, edited by George W. Wenzel, Grete Hovelsrud-Broda, and Nobuhiro Kishigami, pp. 61–86. Osaka: National Museum of Ethnology.

———. 2013. "Inuit and Modern Hunter-Gatherer Subsistence." *Études/Inuit/Studies* 37(2):181–200.

West, Paige. 2016. *Dispossession and the Environment: Rhetoric and Inequality in Papua New Guinea.* New York: Columbia University Press.

Weston, Kath. 1997 [1991]. *Families We Choose: Lesbians, Gays, Kinship.* Revised, 2nd edition. New York: Columbia University Press.

Wilson, Waziyatawin Angela and Michael Yellow Bird, eds. 2005. *For Indigenous Eyes Only: A Decolonization Handbook.* Santa Fe: School of American Research.

Wolcott, Harry F. 2005. *The Art of Fieldwork.* Lanham: Rowman & Littlefield.

———. 2008. *Ethnography: A Way of Seeing.* Lanham: AltaMira Press.

Wolken, Jonathan. 2008. Interview, Jonathan Wolken—Author, Washington Depot, CT., August 6, 2008.

Wulff, Helena. 2002. "Yo-yo Fieldwork: Mobility and Time in a Multi-Local Study of Dance in Ireland." *Anthropological Journal on European Cultures* 11:117–36.

Young, Iris Marion. 1990. *Justice and the Politics of Difference.* Princeton: Princeton University Press.

Zeleza, Paul Tiyambe. 2019. "Africa's Persistent Struggles for Development and Democracy in a Multipolar World." *Canadian Journal of African Studies/Revue Canadienne des Études Africaine* 53(1):155–70.

Zhang, Jinhong. 2014. *Puer Tea: Ancient Caravans and Urban Chic.* Seattle: University of Washington Press.

Zimmer-Tamakoshi, Laura, ed. 2018. *First Fieldwork: Pacific Anthropology 1960-1985.* Honolulu: University of Hawai'i Press.

Index

"fair trade," 7

Falzon, M.A., 131

family: conversations about, 119–20; creating an anthropological, 99–121; ethnographers become, 66; idea of host "family," 102–4; Inuit *ilagiit* networks, 81–82, 84, 89–94, 96; Kalsrap's discourse on, 113–17; long-distance relationships, 113; Marta on capitalists and, 7; meaning for research participants, 102; paying one's, 86; personal relationships in fieldwork, xiv, xvi, 104–7; power and protection in, 112; reciprocity in, 108; research participants become like, xii; in research process, 118–19; rules of reciprocity conflict with culturally specific notions of, xvii; Wentworth's discourse on, 110–13. *See also* adoption

family names, 33

Farmer, Paul, 55n2

Fatima, 37

Federici, Sylvia, 3

Feld, Steven, 50

feminism: on divergences from normal conditions in science, 17n4; on ethnographic research, 3, 103; on gendered division of labor, 17n2; on power inequalities in fictive kinship, xxi

Ferguson, James, 31, 39, 40, 52

Fernea, Elizabeth Warnock, 20

"Field Research in Local Communities" (course), xi

fieldwork: choreography compared with, 62; cosmology and constraint in transnational, 19–38; courses in, xi, 124–25; dangers and difficulties in, 102, 103; debts incurred in, 9, 15; decolonizing, 120; exchange in, 4; idea of host "family" in, 102–4; in Juchitán, Oaxaca, 57–78; learning in the field, 61–62; long-term, xii–xxi, 40–41, 57, 65–68,

86, 94, 102, 106, 131; memoirs, 124, 125, 128; multitemporal, 32; personal relationships in, xiv, xvi, 104–7; rethinking from relational perspective, 3–4; returning to the field, xvii, 32–33, 36; separation between keyboard and field, 10; what it is and what to expect, 60–61; write everything down, 59. *See also* research

Fienup-Riordan, Ann, 87

Fisher, John: on anthropologists as scorpions, 2, 125; on anthropologists' debt as a life's work, 16, 125; on anthropologists' expertise, 16, 123–24; on capitalists seen as scorpions, 2, 126; in Center for Sustainable Development–Génesis cooperative conflict, xix, 11–13, 15–16; cited, 2, 4, 7, 11, 12; financial relationship with Marta, 10; parents' bankruptcy, 9, 10–11, 15; as technical director of workshop, 8; works with Génesis cooperative, 8–9; years of engagement of, 125

Flinn, Juliana, 104, 106

Fluehr-Lobban, Carolyn, xii, xix

Fonoti, Rochelle Tuitagava'a, 107

food: "country" foods, 84–86; gifts of, 34, 72, 87; insecurity in Canadian Arctic, 94; in Inuit rules of reciprocity, 81; kola nuts, 23, 24, 25, 27, 28; *totopos, 69*, 70, 71, 76; in Vanuatu, 99, 111, *112*, 116

Forrest, Joshua, 21, 31

forty-day mass (*misa de 40 días*), 72–73

Foucault, Michel, 48

Fourshey, Catherine Cymone, 38n2

Franklin, Sarah, 132n4

Freeman, Milton M.R., 87

Freire, Paul, 7, 48

friends: Carrier's definition of friendship, xvii; compensation and friendship, xviii; efforts at friendship feel inadequate, xvii; beyond

About the Editors and Contributors

Michelle C. Johnson is Professor of Anthropology at Bucknell University. A cultural anthropologist specializing in religion and ritual in Africa and the contemporary African diaspora, she has conducted extensive fieldwork in Guinea-Bissau and with Guinean immigrants in Portugal. She has held grants from the Social Science Research Council, the U.S. Department of Education (Fulbright-Hays), and the Woodrow Wilson Foundation. In 2019, she was awarded Bucknell University's 1956 Lectureship for Inspirational Teaching. Her articles have appeared in the *Journal of Religion in Africa*, *African Studies Review*, *Anthropology Quarterly*, and *Food and Foodways*. She is the author of *Re-making Islam in African Portugal: Lisbon—Mecca—Bissau* (2020, Indiana University Press).

Edmund (Ned) Searles is Professor of Anthropology and Chair of the Department of Sociology and Anthropology at Bucknell University. He continues to conduct ethnographic research among Inuit in Canada. His research specializations include hunting and subsistence, ethnicity and cultural identity, and local responses to food insecurity in the Canadian Arctic. His articles have appeared in *Anthropology and Humanism*, *Études/Inuit/Studies*, *Food and Foodways*, and *Hunter Gatherer Research*. At Bucknell he teaches the anthropology of Native North America, environmental anthropology, and the anthropology of place. He is currently writing a book on the cultural dimensions of place and identity among Nunavut Inuit.

* * *

Josh Fisher is Associate Professor of Anthropology at Western Washington University. He edits the *Anthropology of Work Review*, a journal of the Society for the Anthropology of Work and the American Anthropological Association. His research in Nicaragua concerns the collaborative economies and ecologies of community development and urban environmental change. His recent project, "Proyecto Buen Vivir," involves a series of experimental, collaborative workshops with a cohort of forty participants from various sectors of Ciudad Sandino, Nicaragua. These experiments present new opportunities for collaborative ethnography as well as for considering the role that anthropology might play in addressing the challenges of urban community development and environmental change.

Alma Gottlieb is Professor Emerita of Anthropology at the University of Illinois at Urbana-Champaign, and Visiting Scholar in Anthropology at Brown University. A past president of the Society for Humanistic Anthropology, she has (co-)authored or (co-)edited nine books and dozens of articles and has pioneered several disciplinary directions, including ethnographic writing, the anthropology of menstruation, and the anthropology of infancy. Her research and writing have focused on Côte d'Ivoire and, more recently, Cape Verde and the global Cape Verdean diaspora, with support from the John Simon Guggenheim Foundation, the Social Science Research Council, the National Endowment for the Humanities, and the Wenner-Gren Foundation. She blogs about contemporary issues at https://almagottlieb.com and maintains a public Facebook page for her latest coedited book, *A World of Babies,* at https://www.facebook.com/WOBBook.

Julie Kalsrap is a mother from Pango Village, Efate, Vanuatu. She is married with three children, two boys and one girl. She likes to sew and contribute to community programs that support the improvement and development of her community. Her main focus and goal in her life is to take good care of her children to ensure that they grow up to be caring people for the future.

Carolyn M. Rouse is Professor and Chair of the Department of Anthropology at Princeton University. Her research focuses on race and inequality in religion, medicine, education, and economic development. She is the author of *Engaged Surrender: African American Women and Islam* (2004, University of California Press) and *Uncertain Suffering: Racial Healthcare Disparities and Sickle Cell Disease* (2009, University of California Press), and she is co-editor (with John L. Jackson and Marla F. Frederick) of *Televised Redemption: Black Religious Media and Racial Empowerment* (2016, NYU Press). She is currently completing her most recent book, *Development Hubris: Adventures Trying to Save the World.*

Anya Peterson Royce is Chancellor's Professor of Anthropology and Comparative Literature at Indiana University. She is also Adjunct Professor at the University of Limerick, where she was awarded an Honorary Doctorate in 2010. She specializes in the anthropology of dance and performing arts, identity, pilgrimage, and ethnography of Mexico, especially the Isthmus Zapotec people of Juchitán with whom she has worked since 1968. In 2016, she received the Medal of the Zapotec People for her contributions to the community. She has curated three exhibits of her photographs of the Isthmus Zapotec in Juchitán and at Indiana University. In 2018, Mexico's Arts and Culture channel used her and her husband Ronald's photographs in a series of documentaries about Juchitán. She has published numerous articles and chapters, three edited volumes, and six books, including *Becoming an Ancestor: The Isthmus Zapotec Way of Death* (2011, SUNY University Press).

Chelsea Wentworth is a research fellow in the Department of Community Sustainability at Michigan State University. Her research interests include food security and access, public health nutrition, critical medical anthropology, gender inclusive development programs, and visual research methods. She works in Flint, MI and Allegheny County in the United States. Since 2009, she has conducted ethnographic research in Vanuatu in collaboration with the Vanuatu Cultural Centre and the Vanuatu Ministry of Health. Her international and U.S.-based research emphasize feminist community-engaged research praxis and understanding food access through a systems-based approach. She has received funding from the U.S. Fulbright Program, the Foundation for Food and Agriculture Research, and the Hewlett Foundation. Her publications appear in *Anthropological Forum, Medical Anthropology, The Asia Pacific Journal of Anthropology, Food and Foodways*, and in several community-engaged outreach documents.